# FACTORS INFLUENCE ORGANIZATIONAL BEHAVIOR

JOHN LOK

# Contents

# Preface

Preface

I write the book aim to let any working people learn how to dealt personnel challenges when who need to cooperate with their staffs. I shall use different working environments to suppose what the personnel challenges you will face and I also suggest that you ought adopt what personnel solvable methods and positive attitudes to solve these personnel challenges are the best. I shall indicate different organizations' staffs cooperation challenges and I also suggest my best personnel solvable methods to dealt these challenges, for example, movie making team, baseball team, nuclear factory, business office, university, interior decorating partnership , bank, restaurant etc. different organizations. This book is suitable to be read by managers, CEO, administration clerk, organizational psychology etc. professional.

Can time pressure management raise employee individual or team efficiency or inefficiency? In what suitation, time pressure can raise efficiency productivity? How can improve efficiency? It depends on raising bonus, salary, raising welfare, building good relationship between employers and employees or other factors to improve efficiency in more time pressure working environment or less time pressure working environment. I shall indicate some organizational behavioral cases to attempt to explain whether suitable time pressure working environment factor can assist organization to raise efficiency.

I shall indicate Hong Kong labors abnormal long time working hours factor which can influence society economic growth and raises productivity in long time. Why do I choose to research this topic? Because I discovered many employers need labors to increase working hours to work often, such as China , Hong Kong etc. developing countries. Although, they feel this method will help them to reduce to spend salary or wage expenditure to employ extra full time labors to assist them to achieve to raise aim of productivity. But in fact, they neglect to consider other disadvantages to cause their labors to feel tiring and unfair treatment and reduce their stanrdard of life, due to their labors will not increase salary or wage very much and who also need to work very long hours per working day. I shall indicate evidences to prove why abnormal work hours method can only raise productivity in the short term, but this method can not raise productivity in the long term and it can also influence overall society economic decline and it can also influence labors' standard of life to be poor. In the final, I shall also recommend how employers, such as Hong Kong and China employers how to change their methods to achieve to raise their productivity in the long term. This book is suitable to any employers to read when who have interest to learn how to raise their workers' productvity in the long term.

In this book I aim to research whether time factor can influence the consumer individual consumption desire to be changed either to choose to buy this product or consume this service or choose to buy another product or consume another service to replace the consumer whose original preference choice. If time factor can influence any one consumer individual consumption choice to be changed easily.

# Prologue

behavioral changes and marketing
behavioral changes.
　· How to apply behavioral economy
theory to predict marketing
behavioral changes more accurate? P.81-111
　· How to apply behavioral economy
theory to understand and manage
people within organizations?
　　　Bibliography
　　　Behavioral economic method
predicts stable basic income
consumer individual spending
behavior
　· How to apply behavioral
economic method to
contribute to the stable basic
income target consumer group's
consumption prediction?
　· How to apply behavioral
economic method to
predict labor market changing
behavior ?

How can apply behavioral
economy method raises basic
stable income consumer
consumption desire
　　　1. Basic stable income consumption
great of small amount desire
2. Life-cycle advertisement method prediction of consumer behavior
3. Raising electricity consumption
from electricity user individual habit
　　　Consumer confidence is as a
predictor of consumption spending
　· What is confidence in consumption survey ?
　· What is a confidence indicator ?

How to apply behavioral
economy methods influence employee individual psychology to achieve
raise productivity of long term
incentive intention?
　· Increasing salary is short term incentive productivity method
　　· How to improve the design of
incentive structures to encourage productivities organizations?
　· Building employees and managers
kindly co-operational relationship
method
　· Can bonus method encourage
service performance to be raised ?
　· Economic views of human
motivation nature

Under-level productive efficiency
and low-consumption desire
behavioral economic influences

Chapter 6
Consumer behavioral factors
influence theory
　How and why time limiting pressure
influences consumer choice p.112-160
　How the time consumption pressure
factor influences irrational
consumption decision making

Time pressure consumption decision
making process characteristics

Reducing time pressure consumption
methods

What are the in-store and out-store
factors influence supermarket
fast moving consumer decision

What consumption is most
influenced in preference choice
by time pressure

Time pressure impacts consumer
behavioral effect
    · The reasons cause consumers
feel time pressure

May time dominate consumption
final purchase decision making

Methods avoid consumers
feel time pressure

Time press how influences
video playing game consumer
purchase behavior

Time pressure consumption or
production situation explanation

# CHAPTER ONE

# Employee psychological rational work behavior

Why does the employee choose to do whose behavior to perform in the working environment? What are the general factors to cause his behavioral performance to bring his job performance effect in the working environment? In simple, I shall indicate some factors to explain how and why they can influence employee individual chooses to perform his behavior in any working environment in generally, These factors will influence how the employee perform his behavior and why he performs his behavior when he feels his behavior or peformance is more satisfactory to his organizational demand or need. Then, I shall indicate some different organizational cases to attempt to explain why and how these factors cause the employee performs his behavior in his organization as below chapters.

Firstly, I shall indicate different factors can influence why and how the employee decide to do his performance in any organizations in generally as below:

(1) Organizational causing factor

What does one organization mean? An organization means human creations, rather than buildings, equipment,machinery etc. It can include industrial, commercial , educational, medical , social clubs, etc. different kinds of organizations. In general, staffs within any organizations will feel need to work to achieve the organizational goals, and co-ordinate their activities for any missions. Each department's staff individual behavior or performance have relationship to be influenced by structures, informal or unofficial groups and structures can be at least as important as the formal organization structure. So, it seems that any different organizational structures will influence their staffs' behavior or performance indirectly or directly. Each employee will have one unique or idenified role in the organization. " The roles people play rather than the personalities in the roles" ( Perrow, 1970, p.2). So, each staff will feel or he will know what will be his role playing and the interrelationships between organizational structure and role playing factors , they can cause how each staff decides or chooses how any why he ought need to do his behavior in order to adapt his organization's working environment need or demand.

In general, in bureaucratic model of organizations, where work is organized and conducted on an entirely rational basis, such as government's any departments, which are usually bureaucratic model of organizations. The essential features of a bureaucracy are: Specialization of division of labour , a hierarchy of authority, written rules and regulations, writting memos or notices for any tasks message, reports are more needed more than oral message to be communication channels within the organization's different departments' coordination. Hence, in bureaucratic , staff individual will consider to do any tasks or perform whose behavior carefully in order to avoid error occurrence, or is encountered complains by clients or same level staffs or his supervisor or manager within himseld department. So, organizational structure factor will influence how and why its employee decides to do behavior or performance when he feels his behavior is more rational or suitable to adapt him organization's need or demand.

(2) Staff individual work psychological factor

Miller ( 1966) explains psychology means what the science of mental life. Mental life refers to three phenomena: behaviors, thoughts and emotions. However, in any organizations, employees will have any characteristics of work psychology to influence whose performance or behavior in any working environment. For example, when the employee feels stressed, he will feel thoughts and emotion to be negative or poor as well as he also feels fear the he can not finish his tasks to let his supervisor or manager feels unhappy or he will complain his working performance is inefficient , even he will dismiss him on the day or later. Then, his fear emotion will influence he may not cooperate with his other same level of staffs in their team easily. It is one good feeling stresses at work case explains how and why the employee will perform worse or poor level suddenly in any organizations. For another example, when a group of staffs need to make decisions, and the extent to which, a person's attitudes towards particular groups of staffs can influence his or her behavior towards them within the department. The organization's team leaders, e.g. manager, supervisor, CEO, he/she will need have good emotion managing ability and managing ability to perpare how to manage his/her teams to cooperate work together in any teams efficiently. In this high stress working environment, the high stress feeling employee will need to judge how to do his behavior in order to manage his teams work together efficiently daily. Hence, some attention is also paid to defining how situations differ from each other psychologically. The high level leader or CEO position managing staff will need to know the supervisor or manager's personality and psychological characteristics tendency how to influence their behavior, think and feel in certain ways in order to let he/she has more confidence to manage the different departments' managers or supervisors more easily , such as the CEO, the top level leader. So, the top level, CEO needs have good work psychological knowledge to know how to manage his/her middle level, such as mangers , supervisors more easily. Then, he /she may have more confidence to manage whose organization efficiently and effectively. So, when the top level employee , such as CEO can know every middle and low level manager or supervisor individual personality characteristics factor. Then, he/she can increase more confidence to know how to manage each department, each team in low and middle level organization structure more efficiently and effectively. So, the working psychological factor will influence how and why the top, middle and low level employees how any why decide their choice to do their performance or behavior in consequently. For example, it is usually that when the employee feels how job satisfaction, then he will choose to perform worse working behavior because he feels that his manager does not consider what kinds of tasks are his interesting jobs. So, his dissatisfaction will influence his working performance to be poor or worse to compare his prior working performance when he feels more bored or low dissatisfaction to himself tasks. Then, his dissatisfactory job feeling will influence his emotion to be worse or poor as well as he will perform more worse or behaves more worse in order to let his manager or supervisor to feel. It is possible that he wants to use worse working performance or worse working attitude to let his manager or supervisor to know his job dissatisfactory or bored feeling. Then, he can encourage his manager or supervisor to change other new and interesting tasks to let him to attempt to replace current bored tasks in possible.

(3) The social and economic factor

Iles and Robertson ( 1989) have recently pointed out that there has been relatively little work in personal selection which has looked at the issues involved from the perspective of candidates. The only candidate-centred area of work which features extensively in the personnel selection research literature concerns the extent to which selection procedures are fair to different sub-groups usually ethic minorities or women of the population. A large amount of research material focusing on this issue has seen produced. A variety of terms such as bias, adverse, impact, fairness and differential validity are used in the literature or this issue and a clear grasp of the meanings and definitions of some of these terms of some of these terms is crucial to an understanding of the research results.

Hence, when one staff feels that his manager or supervisor is often treated to let he feels unfair or biases simply to compare the other members of different sub-groups in whose team. Then, his unfair treatment feeling how and why to choose or decide to perform whose working behavior to be worse to compare his prior working performance or behavior So, the unfair feeling treatment factor will influence the employee chooses to perform poor or worse working behavior or working performance, because general employee usually feels that it is one important channel to let his supervisor or manager to know his any job-related unfair feeling emotion is caused by the impact of unfair personnel selection procedures factor influence.

Normally, of cours, the extent to which a fair selectin method is related to job performance, it means that when the employee feels that manager or supervisor can let him to compete to do this job in fair selection method as well as he can earn more reasonable or fair salary to compensate whose job ability . Then, he will attempt to perform better in order to satisfy his manger or supervisor's job demand. Otherwise, if he feels that he can not earn the higher salary level, due to that he needs to do the lower level job -related task unfairly, but in fact, he believes that he have ability to do another better position and earn more salary in this organization. Then, he will perform worse to complain whose organizational unfair selection treatment to him.

So, the reasonable and fair personnel selection procedures on candidates factor will influence the organization's any staff individual performance. In consequently, all of these factors will influence how any why some staffs perform worse or better. Then, I shall inficate some cases to let readers to attempt to judge whether which of above these factors can cause these organizations' employees to choose or decide to perform their behaviors in their organizations in order to adapt their working environment easily. You can learn to judge whether time pressure is the main factor to cause your organization's employee individual performance to be worse or any other main factors accurately.

Reference

Iles, P. A. and Robertson, I.T. (1989) . The impact of personnel selection procedures on candidates. In Herriot, P. ( Ed.), Assessment and selection in organizations. Chichester: John Wiley.

Miller, G.A. ( 1966) . Psychology: The science of mental life. Harmondsworth: Penguin.

Perrow, C. (1970). Organizational Analysis. Belmont, Calif: Wadsworth.

Long time working hours how influence
marketing consultant team
cooperation

Whether this marketing consultant organization ought need to reduce time pressure to let marketing consultants to cooperate to finish any marketing research projects before due date more easily? Describe people related problems or issues, one marketing consultant firm, Ann Wood faced personnel problem during the day. Ann Wood, marketing director faced problem of two senior marketing analysts would leave her marketing research department as well as after these two senior market analysts left her department, it would cause the one urgent and important market analysis was delayed and it was more difficult to finish before the due date. Ann Wood, her marketing research manager, Joe would lack these two senior market analysts continue to assist whose marketing department to help to finish this one important market analysis during the date. The result of the one important market analysis was delayed to finish after the due date. Ann Wood would face her employer felt who could not achieve excellent performance to promote to do this marketing director position to manage her marketing research department to operate successfully. Even, after these two senior marketing analysists decided to leave Ann, marketing director her marketing department during the day. This issue would influence the overall many teams of other marketing analysts and senior marketing analysts who lost more confidence to serve Ann Wood's marketing department to cause it would have many marketing analysts and senior marketing analysts would plan to leave her department after her first working day. However, the major factor caused these two senior marketing analysts decided to leave her department during the day, it is possible that because their office computers were broken down, so they could not use internet to send this important marketing analysis project to let their manager and Ann, marketing director to read by email during the day or they felt their salaries level were below than marketing salary level, so they had planned to leave during Ann wood her first work day . During the day, the reasons of these two senior marketing analysts who planned leaving include that they felt who were very talented in whose job and had won several key projects as proof, so who ought earn higher salary, During the day, after their leaving, some other marketing analysts also planned to leave because who felt these two senior marketing analysts leaving, then they would rise workloads rapidly and they felt the marketing salaries level were higher than their current salaries unfairly. Hence, Ann Wood would face some marketing analysts and senior marketing analysts would leave her department during the day.

Suggestion of time pressure reducing method

Did the marketing consultant can handle to finish any marketing research project in team effectively before due date, when she feel to work in one reducing time pressure working environment?

I think she did not handle effectively in these people related matters. An effective senior manager needs to spend much time talking with insiders and outsiders about vision, strategy, and other major issues to the direction of the organization. A senior leader needs to make the strategic decision for the firm. Skills in conceptualizing, communicating and understanding the perspectives of others are critical for these discussion. A senior manager also needs spend time helping middle managers to define and redefine their roles and to manage conflict because middle managers are often central to the organization's communication networks. Skills in listening, conflict management, negotiating and motivating are important for these activities. Ann Wood ought attempt to use these methods to handle her staffs personal problems effectively.

Engagement is as the extent to which staffs enjoy and believe in what who do and feel valued for doing it. So, if they feel enjoyment, her staffs tend to receive more pleasure and satisfaction from what who do if who are in jobs or roles that match both their interests and skills. For example, some people like jobs that require travel enjoyment, when some prefer not to travel. Others like a high risk/high reward bonus plan where others prefer a more stable and predictable salary. Some individuals like work in a team environment, others like work more independently. So, Ann Wood ( head of marketing ) can make questionnaires to enquire every project team members what non financial and financial rewards are who want to get from this employer in order to raise their efficiency to work and reduce the leaving staff numbers in every project team.

In belief, if her staffs felt who were making meaningful contributions to their jobs, their current employer and society. Then, who should tend to be more engaged to the connection between what every project team does every day and the goals and mission of Ann Wood's company can be engaged successfully. Other people related problem is Ann's staffs lack enough marketing research skill and working experience. For example, Ann's one of staff Joe Jackson, the current manager of the market research group, who complained to Ann about the company's intranet had been down about half of the night and this technical problem had prevented timely access to data from a central server, resulting in a delay in the completion of an important market analysis on her first work day. He could not attempt to find any department staffs to help him to solve this problem. He did not know that whose some marketing research projects should delay if who waited Ann arrived office and then enquired her how to solve. Moreover, every marketing team members who ought lack enough marketing research working skills because who have no anyone could have confidence to finish every important and urgent marketing research projects before due date. Otherwise, if they had specialised marketing research skill, they ought spend little time to finish these urgent and important projects. So, the computer technical problem would not influence their projects to be finish. Thus Ann would face that many staffs will leave her department and the important and urgent marketing research projects will be delayed to finish after the due date.

What do I believe she should have done when she feels that she is working in one time pressure reducing working environment?

On the one hand, Ann only believed Joe, the current manager of the market research group whose suggestions to increase the market analysts salary if she want to increase their speed to finish every marketing research analysis and reducing the market analysts turnover numbers. She had not enquire other different marketing research managers idea why they could not finish every marketing research project quickly. What the problems were caused who are encountered to finish every marketing research project slowly.

On the other hand, Ann could not know what the urgent jobs are who ought need to solve. When Joe, the current manager of the market research group told her that the company's intranet has been broken to cause a delay in the completion of an important market analysis. After she had not attempted to find the computer technical staffs to help her to repair intranet during the day and she still to read any email in her office computer during the day.

I think Ann needed to attempt to find computer technical staffs to help her to repair intranet immediately and she ought not spend much time to see email, she ought continue enquire whether intranet had been repaired and the completion of an important market analysis had been sent during the day and she ought not spend much time to discuss to increase salaries matter to market analysts with Joe during the day. Thus, Ann did not know what the duties are needed to handle urgently during the day effectively.

Is Ann Wood a high involvement manager, due to Ann often feel time pressure to work? provide evidence.

I feel that Ann Wood is not a high involvement manager. From the motivational and leadership practices of managers to the internal dynamic of employee-based teams to the values that provide the base for the organization's culture, successful firms develop approaches that unleash the potential of their people ( human capital). However, Ann Wood does not understand the actions of every team individual member and every team group in her marketing research department as well as who also does not understand the actions focused on acquiring, developing, and applying the knowledge and skills of every team members as well as who lacks an approach that involved organizing and managing every team's knowledge and skill effectively

to implement her marketing research department's strategy and gains a competitive advantage. Thus, if Ann, head of marketing director could organize and manage every marketing research team effectively, the knowledge and skills of every marketing research team member in the marketing research department can drive sustainable competitive advantages and long term financial success. For example, Ann's one of staff Joe Jackson, the current manager of the market research group, who complained to Ann about the company's intranet had been down about half of the night and this technical problem had prevented timely access to data from a central server, resulting in a delay in the completion of an important market analysis on her first work day. He could not attempt to find any department staffs to help him to solve this problem. He did not know that whose some marketing research projects should delay if who waited Ann arrived office and then enquired her how to solve. Moreover, every marketing team members who ought lack enough marketing research working skills because who have no anyone could have confidence to finish every important and urgent marketing research projects before due date. Otherwise, if they had specialised marketing research skill, they ought spend little time to finish these urgent and important projects. So, the computer technical problem would not influence their projects to be finish. I think she did not handle effectively in these people related matters.

An effective senior manager needs to spend much time talking with insiders and outsiders about vision, strategy, and other major issues to the direction of the organization. A senior leader needs to make the strategic decision for the firm. Skills in conceptualizing, communicating and understanding the perspectives of others are critical for these discussion. A senior manager also needs spend time helping middle managers to define and redefine their roles and to manage conflict because middle managers are often central to the organization's communication networks. Skills in listening, conflict management, negotiating and motivating are important for these activities. On the one hand, Ann only believed Joe, the current manager of the market research group whose suggestions to increase the market analysts salary if she want to increase their speed to finish every marketing research project and reducing the market analysts turnover numbers. She had not enquire other different marketing research managers idea why they can not finish every marketing research project quickly. What the problems are that who are encountered to cause to finish every marketing research project slowly. On the other hand, Ann could not know what the urgent jobs are who ought need to solve. When Joe, the current manager of the market research group told her that the company's intranet has been broken to cause a delay in the completion of an important market analysis. After she had not attempted to find the computer technical staffs to help her to repair intranet during the day and she still to read any email from her office computer during the overtime of the whole day. It proved that her time management is not effective to deal what the jobs are urgent and what the jobs are not urgent to do during the day.

If no, how well do you think she will perform better in her new job as head of marketing , if she can work in one time pressure reducing working environment?

I think Ann needed to attempt to find computer technical staffs to help her to repair intranet immediately and she ought not spend much time to see email, she ought continue enquire whether intranet had been repaired and the completion of an important market analysis had been sent during the day and she ought not spend much time to discuss to increase salaries matter to market analysts with Joe during the day. Thus, Ann did not know what the duties are needed to handle urgently during the day effectively. The most important, Ann needs to know what kind of job duties who needs to do as she is director of marketing clearly. This marketing research department is an internal department , every project team leader needs to manage and arrange every team member to finish every marketing research project efficiently and effectively. Hence, Ann's main duty ought to assist her every marketing research team to finish every marketing analysis before the due date to avoid to extend time to finish every important marketing analysis in this marketing department. Ann needs to know individual factors, e.g. learning ability, personality, values, motivation and stress and interpersonal factors, e.g. leadership, communication, decision making skill, intra and inter group
dynamic communications will influence her performance in her new job as director of marketing successfully.

I think Ann Wood ought to perform as these methods in her new job as head of marketing. However, She could attempt to produce a fair job description, it's an internal part of job evaluation process, grading and salary description, training is focused on elements of a job and how employees can perform better in their job. Aim to produce a reasonable salary to compare market salary level in every specific positions. Job analysis is establishing and defining every position correctly is from the starting point. Enquiring employees to complete questionnaires, observing and interviewing people. It aims to enlarge job enrichment, it extends the work of existing employees to cover more responsibility and decision making. Motivation is the act of getting someone to act on a situation in a workplace. Maslow's hierarchy of needs includes these level: The first level is physiological needs are basic needs to be met in order to survive, including food, water, clothing, sleep and shelter. The next level is security, staffs' surroundings are not threatening to them or family. If the environment seems to be safe, then it means stability in the workplace. Security could also include financial security. This could be achieved by creating a retirement package, securing job position and insurance. The third level is affiliation which is the need to feel a since of belonging or to be loved. In the workplace, this means to feel as though they are a part of the group and included in the work. The fourth level is explained as esteem. This is the view that one has of themselves, the person must have a high image of them self and encompass self respect. Feelings of self worth and the need for respect from others. The last and final stages of the hierarchy of needs is self actualization . This level is defined as someone being all they can be and they have met each of the previous stages. The person's talents are being completely utilized. The growth needs or the highest level of needs are the only real motivators of employees. Employees feel dissatisfied, so who unmotivated. For an employee to be true motivated, the employee's job has to be fully enriched where the employee has the opportunity for achievement and recognition, stimulation, responsibility and advancement.

Ann Wood can apply Maslow's hierarchy of needs motivation theory to satisfy whose staffs personal needs. She needs to make her staffs to understand that Ann ( their head of marketing) feels they are important to this company by financial and non financial types of motivation in workplace compensation to them. Ann Wood ( head of marketing) can attempt to implement these types of motivation into her specific new workplace. Her workplaces are suffering with employees who are unmotivated and overall work performance is failing. Currently her employees do not have organizational commitment, then there is no incentive to excel at their own personal goals and organizational goals. If these employees can discuss techniques are implemented in the specific work sites and she needs to make employees have not feel as though who have reached in the end of their career job satisfaction. Thus, her employees feel dissatisfactory to their jobs and they feel financial and non financial rewards are not fair to compare other employers in this market salary level to cause they intend to quit their current employer. She can use quantitative performance measurement to measure her employee work performance, such as absenteeism, project production turnover, extra hours worked as well as qualitative measurement, such as
supervisor/manager ratings on appropriate performance . She can predict

her staffs who feel dissatisfactory to their jobs from these information in order to enquire their needs. Often, the measurement will be used in part depend on what work outcomes are regarded as beneficial by her organization. For example, she can use rating form to evaluate every project team members of every one whose job performance from their marketing manager after every project team has finished its project. In conclusion, I give these suggestions to change her performance to deal her new job as head of marketing. For example: Removing some job controls, increasing worker accountability for them own work, giving workers free choice which projects who have interest to finish early, giving greater job freedom or additional authority to every project team members, making periodic reports directly to every project teams ( not through every project team leader), introducing new and more difficult projects to give to the more potential project team members and assigning specialized projects to more potential project team members to attempt to finish, so who can become experts.

Assume Ann Wood wants her managers and associate to be the foundation for her department's competitive advantages. Use framework summarized to assess the degree to which Ann's people are a source of competitive advantage at the point of time. Competitive advantage means four key attributes: values, rarity, a lack of substitutes, difficult to imitate. Human resources are seen to be valuable, the cost of replacing employees who leave organization is high, who are experienced and are seen by clients as important. It results when an organization can perform some aspect of its work better than competitors or when it can perform the work in a way that competitors can't duplicate. The resource based view of organization theory refers the nature of human resource can be regarded as uniquely valuable to organization because who are a collection of asset ( skills, competencies and experience) and are much more difficult to replicate, unlike other conventional asset, such as land or capital. Rarity is value or be a labour group which is short supply. Organizations have as stable supply of skills in short supply will have a competitive advantage. It is difficult to imitate skilled work of employees, change of services can be available. In instant, self service in restaurant but the market for high quality service by skilled employees are constant growth ( Stredwick . J, 2005).

Human capital rareness means the extent to which the skills and talents of an organization's people are unique in the industry as well as human capital imitability means the extent to which the skills and talents of an organization's people can be copied by other organizations. Thus, Ann needs to employ staffs who are valuable, rare and difficult to imitate. If Ann want to lead her marketing research department efficiently. She needs to ensure every team leader has leadership ability and their marketing research skills and talents are unique in this marketing research industry as well as every team member marketing research skills and talents can not be copied by other competitors.

Thus, aims to assess the degree to which Ann's people are a source of competitive advantage at the point of time, who can follow these steps: Firstly, Ann Wood, head of marketing, who can attempt arrange training program is both quantitatively and qualitatively. Such training provides the base for effective of discretion by every marketing research team member. Reward systems that value in individual and team every project productivity help to encourage the type of behaviour that is desired. Giving responsibility and accountability complement the system. It aims to make every marketing research team member who can believe project should be fulfilling before due date, workplace should be fearless and energized, work and family life should be balanced and every project team leader should serve followers, every project team members should be treated like customers and who should not be afraid to make mistakes. This training program aims to achieve further lower turnover, higher satisfaction and stronger motivation among every project team members.

I feel the degree to which Ann's people are a source of competitive advantage at the point of time is not high. The reasons include as below: For example, Ann's one of staff Joe Jackson, the current manager of the market research group, who complained to Ann about the company's intranet had been down about half of the night and this technical problem had prevented timely access to data from a central server, resulting in a delay in the completion of an important market analysis on her first work day. He could not attempt to find any department staffs to help him to solve this problem. He did not know that whose some marketing research projects should delay if who waited Ann arrived office and then enquired her how to solve. Moreover, every marketing team members who ought lack enough marketing research working skills because who have no anyone could have confidence to finish every important and urgent marketing research projects before due date. Otherwise, if they had specialised marketing research skill, they ought spend little time to finish these urgent and important projects. So, the computer technical problem would not influence their projects to be finish. Hence, I think Ann needs to give them training to raise their marketing research skill if she still hope they can have high degree of competitive abilities to finish every further marketing research projects before due date.

Reference

Stredwick. J, (2005). An Introduction to human resource management. Elsevier Ltd, UK.

# CHAPTER TWO

# Long time working hours how influence nuclear factory team cooperation

Can time pressure influences nuclear factory teams' cooperative performance?

Dan was the supervisor of technical maintenance in the nuclear power facility factory and who had noticed that several of his people were reluctant to follow maintenance procedures. He had been told that the specifications were too complex to understand, that the procedures were often unnecessary,and that the plant engineers did not really appreciate maintenance problems. On the one hand, Dan realized that most of their complaints were just excuses for doing things their own way. On the other hand, Dan did not really know which procedures were important and which were not. That's why

Dan had asked Mary, design engineer to meet with him. Mary, design engineer knew nuclear power plants' procedures are complex and potentially risky and every specification and every procedures had a reason for being there. If Dan, supervisor of technical maintenance ignored one procedure, they might get by with it and nothing happens. But one of them just might do it at the wrong time and it caused serious wrong result in this nuclear power plant. So, Mary needs Dan to explain that they had safety and cost to consider. If they lost expensive equipment how they should lie to pay for it. Dan referred that if they lost a finger or got exposes to much radiation, they would not like that happened either.However, Mary needed Dan to follow her specification and procedures to do, but Dan told Mary this really wasn't what his maintenance staffs wanted and they hoped for a little flexibility and who felt who would not like it, but they would have to do it. Lately that afternoon, Dan decided to met his unit and relayed the instructions and who reminded them of the rules and disciplinary actions for not following procedures. At the end of the meeting, who couldn't decide whether whose decision had done any better than Mary's decision. Harry, technical maintenance staff noticed that he had been assigned the routinely scheduled maintenance on the three feed water pumps. The pumps were normally used only for start up and shutdown and as emergency backup. When the main feed water system malfunctioned, these pumps would activate to keep the steam generator from drying out. The procedure also specified that the pumps should be serviced and test one at a time and that one pump should be out of service at a time. Harry thought that who needed to take three hours to service the pumps that way, but who could do it in two hours if who shut don together.

Finally, who did not follow specification and procedures to do maintenance job from Mary demand and who decided to shorten the normal three time to two hours to finish this pump maintenance service job. This case indicated that the nuclear power plant maintenance job needed Mary, design engineer and Dan, supervisor of technical maintenance to co-operate to give their opinions to make any important decision to follow the specification and procedures to reduce the incident crisis occurrence to cause serious death to workers and damage to nuclear power plants. However, due to Dan who had noticed that several of his people were reluctant to follow maintenance procedures. He had been told that the specifications were too complex to understand, that the procedures were often unnecessary, and that the plant engineers did not really appreciate maintenance problems. In fact, I believe that the bad result would be caused seriously. Hence, Mary needed Dan to discuss this issue urgently. However, Mary needed Dan to follow her specification and procedures to do, but Dan told Mary this really wasn't what his maintenance staffs wanted and they hoped for a little flexibility and who felt who would not like it, but they would have to do it. It implied that Dan still agreed whose technician opinions and refused to accept Mary's opinion to follow specifications and procedure in the maintenance procedure as well as Dan decided to meet whose technicians to notify them the rules and disciplinary actions either who might choose to follow procedures or who might choose not to follow during their maintenance. Hence, it implied Dan gave whose technicians to choose freely and Dan's attitude was not forced to need them to follow easily. I agreed that Dan handled this decision was not the best way.However, it was not right that Dan made decisions to choose of nuclear power plant maintenance job whether technicians ought follow specifications and procedure from Mary or technicians ought not follow specifications and procedure from maintenance units actions in the short time. Because it would increase Dan, supervising maintenance unit technicians death or hurt chance and nuclear power plant damaging change if whose decision was wrong. So, Dan ought need to spend time to discuss and gather information to evaluate whether Mary or technicians' suggestion was more safe and less cost to work in nuclear power plant for long term benefits in their meeting together.

In fact, Dan had not follow the correct steps to make final decision before he accepted whose maintenance units did not need to follow specifications and procedures during who needed to maintain nuclear power plant. The decision making steps include that as defining the maintenance problem, e.g. what maintenance problems were the most important to need technicians followed all specifications and procedures to carry on working; identifying criteria, gathering and evaluating information, e.g. other nuclear power plant maintenance procedure methods; listing and evaluating information; selecting best alternative; implementing and following up and giving feedback to let Mary to know the reason either why who disagreed Mary's suggestion or why who agreed whose maintenance units suggestion or none of final decision was made that Mary and Dan and technicians needed to carry on meeting to discuss clearly. An effective decision was as one that was timely, that was acceptable to those affected by it, and that satisfied the key decision criteria, and it was in the systematic and logical process. Mary and Dan and maintenance units had not ever sat down to discuss this issue in any once meeting together. Dan only met Mary and Dan only met maintenance units individual to discuss this issue separately.He did not give chance to let them to discuss with him in meeting room by face to face contact.

Hence, they could not have complete knowledge about all possible alternatives to achieve their potential results effectively because who lacked enough time to make decision making and one good decision making needs a cognitive activity that relies on both perception and judgement. If two people used different approaches to solve problem in the processes of perception and judgement, they were likely to make quite different decision, even if the facts and objectives are identical. As Mary and Dan used different approaches to solve maintenance procedure problem in the process of perception and judgement to decide decision whether the maintenance units needed to follow specifications and procedure or they did not need to follow during technicians did maintenance job in nuclear power plant. Thus, Dan could not ensure technicians' decision whether which was better than Mary's decision because who lacked complete knowledge about all possible alternatives to make final decision before. In conclusion, Dan ought spend time to follow correct decision steps to make decision and who also needed to give them to discuss this issue by face to face contact in meeting and he ought not own objective judgement to agree any one suggestion, who ought give them to make subjective judgement to discuss to accept whose decision freely. Hence, Dan ought to be one participant role and ought not be one controller role in this decision making procedure.

suggestion of time pressure reducing method:

Analyze the critical problem in Part A of the case.

Did Dan handle it in the best way?

What decision styles did he use?

Decisions are reflected the person's preference for one of two perceptual styles and one of two judgement styles. Dan seemed to use intuition style decision, who disliked details and time required to sort and interpret them and whose decision made using this style was based on imagination and Dan believed that whose creativity could help Mary and technicians both to choose whose decision was more suitable. For example, Dan did not spend time to follow decision steps to make decision and Dan did not let Mary and maintenance units and him had chance to meet to discuss this issue by face to face contact to decide whether whose decision was less risky and logical to maintenance units work in nuclear power plant easily. Dan was also a feeling style person to make whose judgement. A feeling style meant a decision style focused on subjective evaluation and the emotional reactions of others. Dan preferred to rely on whose emotions and personal subjective judgements to agree maintenance units' decision. At the earlier, Dan had noticed that several of his people were reluctant to follow maintenance procedures. He had been told that the specifications were too complex to understand, that the procedures were often unnecessary, and that the plant engineers did not really appreciate maintenance problems. So, Dan had accepted maintenance units' suggestion to make judge and Dan had not think and analysed their suggestion clearly. So, Dan chose maintenance units decision was based their feeling and emotion reactions. Before,Dan was met to enquire whose suggestion from Mary. Dan would not accept her suggestion easily, even Mary let Dan to know what the serious crisis would have more chance to occur if his maintenance units did not follow specifications and procedure during they were carrying on maintaining job. However, Dan had not change to accept maintenance units' suggestion easily due to they had influenced Dan's feeling and emotion to judge this issue early.

In what important ways is Harry's behaviour different from Marv's when they are feeling to work in time pressure environment?

During the nuclear power facilities occurred problem, Mary and Harry's both behaviour performance could be seemed as these four aspects to evaluate, such as judgement effort and decision making effort and crisis management effort and time management effort aspects.The important ways is Harry's behaviour different from Marv's included as below: Marv Bradbury, technician was working shift time in nuclear power facility plant. In fact, most technicians did not like this shift, but Marv discovered that who enjoyed this job after few months and who also liked sleep in the mornings and many of this co-workers complained his behaviour to influence poor team work. Marv's job in the nuclear power plant was particular important. Marv's primary was to monitor a series of dials and readouts in the control room. In fact, the system was so automatic, so who did not spend much time to do this duty of control and manage this system. However, if the readings indicated some variance in the system whose responsibilities were great, who would needed to do duty of interpret the readings, diagnose the problem as well as who would needed to do initiate corrective actions if the automatic correcting system failed. For two reasons, Marv never worried about his responsibilities because the system was fault free and self correcting and it was a good system with no weaknesses as well as Marv had confidence to understand about the system and he was trained always knew what he had to do in the event of a problem and was capable of doing it. In fact, the system occurred problem and who attempted to solve, but who felt difficult to deal. Hence, Marv felt the system was in serve trouble and decided to phone to get help. Although, who could not solve this system problem, but who knew the result if the systems dried out, the temperature was really going to go up and that the core was going to be damaged. Hence, the nuclear power facilities would cause to damaged.

However, it took minutes to get someone to attempt to solve this system trouble, but it was too late and no one seemed to know what to do.

On judgement effort and decision making effort aspects, Marv's behaviour performance was seemed as team co-operation managed style person. On the one hand, who lacked decision making effort and who could not attempt to solve problem himself and who needed team co-operation to work together to increase confidence to solve problem. On the other hand, who lacked judgement effort to know whether what who ought need to attempt to solve any during crisis occurred. Moreover, Marv also lacked time management and crisis management efforts.

However, Marv needed to wait eight minutes to get someone to attempt to solve this system trouble, but it was late and no one seemed to know what to do. If the technicians took longer time to arrive, even Marv could not phone to contact them successfully. The result would be more poor seriously. It seemed that Marv could not have confidence to continue to maintain this system. Otherwise, if Marv could attempt to maintain, it was possible that the system could be maintained successfully.

Risk at this immediate accident occurrence, it would seem that risk taken by a group should be the same as the average risk that would have been taken by the individual group members acting alone ( himself). Hence, who decided not to do action

to attempt to solve this trouble, who decided to phone other technician team members to wait their arrival after eight minutes to attempt to solve this trouble, but it was too late and no one seemed to know what to do. However, if who could attempt to solve this trouble within eight minutes, it is possible that this trouble would solve from himself alone.

Harry, technical maintenance staff noticed that he had been assigned the routinely scheduled maintenance on the three feed water pumps. The pumps were normally used only for start up and shutdown and as emergency backup. When the main feed water system malfunctioned, these pumps would activate to

keep the steam generator from drying out. The procedure also specified that the pumps should be serviced and test one at a time and that one pump should be out of service at a time.

Harry thought that who needed to take three hours to service the pumps that way, but who could do it in two hours if who shut don together. Finally, who did not follow specification and procedures to do maintenance job from Mary demand and who decided to shorten the normal three time to

two hours to
finish this pump maintenance service job. Two hours later he was done and
he packed up his tools and hurried to get home.

On crisis management and time management effort aspects, Harry's
behaviour performance was seemed as self managed style. He could attempt
to accept risk to decide how to solve problem from himself effort and
who had effort to judge how to deal in any crisis occurrence and time
management. Hence, it could prove who could deal any crisis occurrence
alone and who did not spend time to wait any team members ( technician
group) assistance, although who could not ensure whose decision whether
it was right or wrong.

Hence, it implied who was one confident person.Harry, technical
maintenance staff noticed that he had been assigned the routinely
scheduled maintenance on the three feed water pumps. The pumps were
normally used only for start up and shutdown and as emergency backup.
When the main feed water system malfunctioned, these pumps would
activate to keep the steam generator from drying out. The procedure also
specified that the pumps should be serviced and test one at a time and
that one pump should be out of service at a time. Harry thought that who
needed to take three hours to service the pumps that way, but who could
do it in two hours if who shut don together. Finally, who did not follow
specification and procedures to do maintenance job from Mary demand and
who decided to shorten the normal three time to two hours to finish this
pump maintenance service job. Two hours later he was done and he packed
up his tools and hurried to get home. On judgement and decision making
effort aspects, Harry's behaviour performed who can attempt to judge what
action was possible more right to solve this trouble, although who could
not ensure whose action is right or wrong, who could make decision to
attempt to finish whose job and who felt who would not need to spend
time to wait other team members ( technicians) to make any decision to
work together. Hence, who performed that who was one confident person.
In conclusion, risk exist when the outcome of a chosen course of action
is not certain. Most decisions in business carry some degree of risk. In
choosing between less and more risky options, an individual's risk taking
propensity, or willingness to take chances, often plays a role. Two persons
with different propensities to take risks may make different decisions when
confronted with identical decision situations and information. One who
is willing to face the possibility if loss, for example, may select a riskier

alternative, whereas another person will choose for taking risks. As Harry and Marv who were working in this same nuclear power facility plant, when the crisis occurred, whose performance would have different to decide to cause different result. Due to Harry performed behaviour was more confident and more judgement effort and self managed person who could accept risk to attempt to make decision alone and disregarded whether the result was right or wrong .

Otherwise, Marv performed behaviour was lacked confidence and less judgement effort and team managed person who could not accept risk to attempt to make decision alone and regarded whether the result was right absolutely. Hence, their performance caused the result was also different, as Harry decided to spend two hours to solve the system trouble alone. Although Marv was not sure that Harry's action whether was correct or incorrect and it needed time to wait whether the system would occur trouble again or not. However, Harry had

attempted to finish whose duties. Otherwise, Marv decided to phone to ask technicians to assist whom and they arrived after eight minutes and who attempted to co-operate to work together. But it was too late and no anyone seemed to know what to do and the system trouble would not still be solve. Hence, it was ensure that the system must be existed trouble and Marv decided not to continue to solve this problem individually and it seemed that Marv could not finish whose duties definitely. Otherwise, Harry could attempt to solve this system trouble alone although it needed time to wait. It seemed that Harry, technician had more strategic decision ability and performed better to compare Marv to deal any crisis occurrence in the nuclear power plant and it seemed that who could assist Dan, supervisor technical maintenance in whose team effectively, although the system needed time to wait to confirm whether it was needed to maintain or needed not maintain again after Macv spent two hours to attempt to maintain. However, it seemed that Harry had more judgement and decision making and crisis management and time management efforts to compare Marv to do this technician position in this nuclear power plant.

How might group decision making be applied at the end of Part B when time pressure is reduced to influene team work?

The group decision making might be applied to Marv, technician shift team as below:

In general ,in high involvement organizations, associates participate in many decisions with lower level and middle level managers and where low level and middle level managers participate in decisions with senior level managers as well as teams of associates can also make some decisions without managerial input. In this way, human capital throughout the organization is utilized effectively. However, group decision making is similar in some ways to individual decision making because the purpose of group decision makes to arrive a preferred solution to a problem, the group must use the same

basic decision making steps: such as defining problem, identifying criteria, gathering and evaluating information, listing and evaluating alternative, choosing the best alternatives and implementing it finally. Groups are made up of multiple individual, however, resulting in dynamic and interpersonal processes that make group decision making different from decision making by individual. For instance, some members of the decision group will arrive with their own expectation, problem definition and predetermined solutions. These characteristics are likely to cause some interpersonal problems among group members. Also some members will have given more thought to the decision situation than other members' expectation about what is to be accomplished may differ. Thus, a group leader may be more concerned with a collection of individuals into a collaborative decision making team than with the development of individual decision making skills.

In fact, group processes that occur during decision making often prevent full decision of facts and alternatives. Group norms, member roles, dysfunctional communication pattern, and too much cohesiveness may deter the group to produce ineffective decisions.

Marv Bradbury, technician was working shift time in nuclear power facility plant. In fact, most technicians did not like this shift, but Marv discovered that who enjoyed this job after few months and who also liked sleep in the mornings and many of this co-workers complained his behaviour to influence poor team work. Marv's job in the nuclear power plant was particular important. His primary was to monitor a series of dials and readouts in the control room. In fact, the system was so automatic, so who did not spend much time to do this duty of control and manage this system. However, if the readings indicated some variance in the system whose responsibilities were great, who would needed to do duty of interpret the readings, diagnose the problem as well as who would need to do initiate corrective actions if the automatic correcting system failed. For two reasons, Marv never worried about his responsibilities because the system was fault free and self

correcting and it was s good system with no weaknesses as well as Marv had confidence to understand about the system and he was trained always knew what he had to do in the event of a problem and was capable of doing it. One day, the system occurred problem and who attempted to solve, but who felt difficult to deal. Hence, Marv felt the system was in serve trouble and decided to phone to get help. Although, who could not solve this system problem, but who knew the result if the systems dried out, the temperature was really going to go up and that the core was going to be damaged. Hence, the nuclear power facilities would cause to damaged. However, I felt that it was wrong decision that Marv decided to phone to technicians to wait eight minutes to attempt to find them to solve this system trouble, but it was too late and no one seemed to know what to do. In the beginning, Marv could attempt to solve this system trouble by individual decision, but then who decided

to phone to technician team members to assist who because who wanted to reduce whose action risk alone. After eight minutes, these technician team members arrived the nuclear power plant.

Marv did not anticipate any actions finally and Marv did not tell technicians how to attempt to act, so who did not anticipate any group decision among their actions finally. In the result, these technicians group decided to auxiliary pump room and discovered that the three valves were still closed and they decided to open the valves, but it was too late and no one seemed to know what to do. During these technicians group decided to do any actions immediately, their group leader would think to build a positive image ( believing this system trouble could solve immediately) under threat ( nuclear power facilities

would occur damage possibly). Hence, this technician group leader had already failed possibly and who would decide to attempt to maintain this system together and who decided not to enquire Dan, supervisor of technician to assist them immediately. It was possible that who felt time was not enough to wait supervisor assistance or who could attempt to solve by themselves. Because Marv believed that group think decision making was more successful than individual decision making.

Although, group think did not guarantee a better decision but simply increased that likelihood of such a result. When good judgement and discussion were suppressed, the group decision could be more effective to compare to individual decision, Hence, it was possible that , the group decision making could give some benefits to Marv's individual decision making, which included that group decision making could reduce more errors to than Marv's individual decision alone; group decision making could reduce pressure when technicians gave their opinions to solve this system trouble at the same time; members who could been quiet were assumed to be in complete this job together; they could build complex rationales that effectively discount warnings or information that conflict with their thinking; they could reduce chance to cause them to ignore any dangers when they worked at the time and they could discussed any facts, criticisms or evaluations to solve this trouble together at the short time possibly.Hence, it implied that group making decision still had these benefits to compare to Marv's individual making decision.

What alternatives do you use for the time pressure reducing possibility of a similar problem in the future?

In academic decision theory, one fundamental decision rule is that of maximizing expected utility. This is the idea that when company management needs to make a decision and there are different choices, each choice has a set of possible outcome with different probabilities. The problem with this procedures
is that in real life the probabilities and utilities are often different to determine. Of course, if the outcomes are more or less certain. There might be more than one item you like and you might have a hard time to choose just one, but choose any one of choice will be a rational choice. More generally, what we should be when we make decisions is to list the pros and cons of each option available to use ( the reasons supporting the option and the reasons against it). Management then choose the option that on balance has the most reasons in its favour. A good decision process requires all time parts being implemented correctly. For example, Is it clear what we have to decide? What is the most important or urgent decision? Are all the options realistic? Are there other options we should consider? Are we overlooked any good or bad consequences of an option? Is there any special criteria for the decision, we should be aware of?

Have the criteria been applied to time pressure reducing working environment wrongly?

Main reasons why people are failure in their creative idea because failure due to lack of part knowledge and relevant skills and failure of concept and wrong with the initial idea or theory and failure of judgement due to management can have the right idea, but make the wrong decision in executing and developing it and due to failure of attitude and forging a new path where others have not gone before requires courage and the right balance of attitude and due to fear to failure to cause management to abandon an idea before it comes to success.

I recommend that Harry, engineer and Dan, supervisor and Dan's group of normal shift and part time technicians who needed have group discussion to decide what were the serious or common problems as well as whether these system problems which needed to follow specification and procedures

or which needed not to follow specification and procedures during who needed to carry on working daily in this nuclear power plant. Because who should not have enough time to predict or evaluate to judge whether which system troubles issues were serious and which system troubles issues were common to decide whether which needed to follow specification and procedures to carry on maintaining job.

Thus, this decision ought be more fair between Harry and technicians to reduce their conflicts.

However, in this time pressure reducing situation, group decision making ( Harry, engineer and Dan, supervisor of maintenance groups and technicians discussion together) must be better than individual decision making ( Harry, engineer and

Dan, supervisor of maintenance group discussion together).

The group decision making advantage is better quality, or least a significant chance of better quality, particularly when complex decisions are being made. The advantage is based on the fact that groups bring more knowledge and facts to make decision and engage in a richer assessment of alternatives. Other advantages include making better of decisions and greater satisfaction in the organization and personal growth for group members. However, time is one several disadvantages associated with using a group to make a decision. Thus, if they had already discussed this issue to make group decision making before any system troubles existed trouble . Then, these technicians would know whether which system troubles were more serious and which system troubles were common to judge whether either which system troubles needed to follow specification and procedures or which system troubles did not need to follow specification. For example, as the shift time technician, Marv and another full time technician who could not judge whether system troubles were serious or not, so who should felt doubt and difficult whether who ought follow all instruction to finish system maintained work or who ought not follow al instruction to finish system maintained work.

Even, Marv decided to phone to technicians to ask their help. Marv would cause these technicians felt difficult to make group think to make decision in the short time. Group think is a more extreme problem where the pressure to conform hinders critical analysis and creativity, resulting in poor decision making, it might include outsiders who disagree and morality superior. These members are likely to feel more comfortable with each other, but who might also mistakenly perceive themselves as creative. In conclusion, group decision making ought be needed between Harry, engineer and Dan, supervisor of maintenance and technicians before other new system troubles occurred.

# CHAPTER THREE

# Long time working hours how influence electronic assemblies factory team cooperation

Can time pressure influence electronic assemblies factory workers team performance ?

The best ways evaluate to measure what factors are seemed to be influencing this company electronic assemblies products manufactory factory workers team performance.

Firstly, we need to know what kind of methods which can be used to measure team performance, then, we can follow these measurement methods to judge what factors are seemed to be influencing this team performance more actually. Effectiveness and efficiency are the best ways to evaluate team performance. Efficiency is oriented towards successful input transformation into outputs. Effectiveness measures how outputs interact with the economic and social environment and it is being used to reflect overall performance of the team. This company electronic assemblies products manufactory factory team of workers could be evaluated team performance in terms of effectiveness. It's main focus is to achieve team's mission, goals and vision, such as whether how many workers could attempt to finish to wire eight assemblies an hour to meet their one client, Pacific electronic company to know how many assemblies of numbers had been finished to wire currently in order to meet whose Pacific electronic company client shipping schedule or not. At the same time, which value these electronic assembly workers whose performance in terms of their efficiency which relates to the optimal use of resources to achieve the desired output, such as whether how many worker numbers and machine tool numbers would be needed to provide to wire assembly numbers to finish in order to meet whose Pacific electronic company client shipping schedule or not. However, this team performance would have this question ,such as whether there was a difference if this team was effective yet inefficient. Hence, this team would face unprecedented

challenges ( factors) which were seemed to be influencing team performance. The first factor was such as, it's client Pacific electronic company needed shorten time to finish wire assemblies which was the main factor to influence performance, such as this team workers would feel difficult to increase to wire eight assemblies an hour from three assemblies an hour, so who would feel anxiety to meet the shipping schedule to finish whose job and quality of assemblies production could not be satisfied to Pacific electronic company client possibly.

The second factor was such as, this company factory and office team management structural relationship. Usually, high team performance has strong upper management and human resource standards which had been set in place. Because of high team performance expectation, right staffs were being hired to fulfil the positions in order to employees were well aware of the performance measurement and the importance achieve the excellence in their duties.

Due to a high degree level of employee involvement needed to be in the team production process, the entity was awarded with staffs commitment which reduced rotation level and the cost associated with the hiring and training process. Hence, employees who were devoted to the team were well aware of necessary knowledge and skill and experience to create unique solutions for clients. Training can be an essential tool for maintaining and improving the productivity of staffs and relevance of skill. The ongoing shortages of labour and skill, the company should be taking action to reduce the impact of staffs scarcity by training staffs who already had employed.

Development opportunities were provided to motivate staffs by providing them with skill and knowledge enrichment . At the same time, a better skilled, more motivated workforce would help boost competitiveness, improved productivity and increased profit margin. Moreover, this company lacked good team communication relationship, such as Bill, factory team supervisor who only knew whose same workers of team, such as some of workers Dennis and Steve and Jack who would feel difficult because whose workers were supposed to wire three assemblies an hour normally with five years, but who were supposed to do eight assemblies an hour to sudden meet one client, Pacific electronic company client schedule to finish confidently as well as who would feel dissatisfactory, due to whose wages did not increase much more to pay for performance to the optimal compensation currently and these workers lacked enough training to face this sudden change to face this client's demand. Thus, it was possible that to influence whose team performance to be poor due to who could not adapt this sudden change from this client's demand. Due to Bill, electronic factory supervisor had not communicate to face to face to contact to enquire whose workers whether what reasons to cause who would feel difficulties if who needed to increase to finish wire assemblies and attempted to find solved methods due to sudden clients' demand. Hence, Bill could not have knowledge and skill to judge whether the reasons were either the numbers of workers or machines were not enough or both to cause that they would feel difficulties to increase their speed and effort to finish up to eight wire assemblies of numbers to meet this clients' current schedule sudden change demand at this moment.

The third factor was whether this company had effective strategic approaches to this team. A high team performance which maintains five major approaches: They include strategy, customers, leadership, processes and structure , values and beliefs. Strategic approach takes the team to a higher plan of maturity with a vision where the entity is going; customer approach strives for loyalty; leadership approach is associated with management knowledge to transfer the strategy
to employees (teams) level and which will have a direct impact on their behaviour and beliefs and teams' processes and structure and high performance team will strive for implementing innovative policies to support team strategy; the last model is value and belief which translates into team ability to implement the strategy. In fact, this team lacked effective strategic approaches, such as Mr Martin, office manager did not told Bill, electronic factory team supervisor how to lead whose team to a higher plan to maturity with a vision where the entity was going, such as team lacked training or team lacked enough numbers of worker and machine to provide to increase to produce up to eight wire assemblies of numbers to meet this client's schedule shorten change demand to cause this team lacked evaluation to measure every worker individual effort to judge

whether who ought have effort to already to finish more wire assemblies of numbers and who ought increase their wages due to they had more effort to raise more productivity to produce eight assemblies or more numbers. Hence, it caused the effort workers did not like to increase the productivity to meet this client sudden change easily due to who felt unfair treatment to compare the other less effort workers in this team. However, the Pacific electronic company client would lose confidence
to Mr Martin office manager if who could not accept Dave, shop of supervisor suggestion either to add some more incentive bonus to these workers to raise whose productivity or providing training or providing more machine and worker numbers to attempt to assist current workers ability to meet the client's schedule. Otherwise, it would cause this client did not choose to find its help next time again. The important factor was whether this factory supervisor and shop supervisor and office manager who had effective communication to predict how to solve any sudden clients' order change trouble between of them.

However, I think that, Bill factory supervisor lacked effective leadership to whose workers team in this factory, such as it seemed that some workers; Dennis, Steve and Jack who responded to Bill factory supervisor who felt difficulties to wire eight assemblies an hour suddenly. In fact, some of them had confidence to finish who told lie to Bill because Bill, factory supervisor could not be a good leader to know how to lead whose team to wire assemblies efficiently and effectively daily. Thus, Bill's leadership would have a direct impact on team workers behaviour and team performance poorly if Bill could not change whose leadership skill and who needed to facilitate workers team performance rather than to direct the team, due to who was a formal leader to their team. The company lacked value and belief with translated into team ability to implement the strategy, such as Mr Martin, office manager could not communicate with Dave, shop of supervisor and Bill, factory of supervisor by face to face contact to discuss whether how who could raise to produce wire assemblies of numbers during any clients' sudden shorten schedule occurrence before, so it caused this factory workers team had not more confident to increase to produce more eight wire assemblies of numbers one hour due to this clients' schedule sudden shorten change. Otherwise, if who could often to discuss to suggest any methods to raise these factory team productivity, this factory leader, Bill would have enough time to plan already how to lead whose factory team workers to co-operate to raise productivity efficiency and effectively in this shorten schedule.

● suggestion time pressure reducing method

Identify the team norms and goals. Are they compatible with organizational objective when these factory workers feel time pressure is reduced?

What factors are seemed to influence team performance to cause these factory workers feel pressure to work in short time?

I felt that some of this electronic company factory team norms and goals are compatible with organizational objectives in some situations, but some of whose team norms and goals are not compatible with organizational objective in some situation. Norms mean rules or standards that regulate the team's behaviour and providing direction and are part of the team's mental model. When individual team members violate team norms, some type of punishment is usually applied. Although, norms allow teams be function smoothly, who can sometimes be harmful to team members. It is important that teams develop norms that both foster team productivity and performance and promote the welfare of individual members. This company goal was that it's factory team needed to finish identified wire assemblies of numbers to satisfy every business clients to meet whose identified schedules individually.

Hence, Bill, the electronic factory team supervisor who needed to follow Dave, shop of supervisor's instruction to inform whose workers team to finish all wire assemblies of numbers to meet every business client's identified schedule on or before due date. Thus, Bill , factory team supervisor needed to give team norms to let whose team of workers to know whose factory's rules or standards that regulated whose workers teams individually behaviour and providing direction to let them to know when ( what the client schedule date was) and what the wire assemblies of numbers the team which must need to finish to deliver to whose clients by shipping. Hence, this factory's rules and standards regulation could be one part to this factory team's mental models on this aspect to achieve this factory workers team norms were compatible with this organizational objective.

Although, the factory workers team norms allowed them to function smoothly, but Bill, factory supervisor could sometimes be harmful to the factory workers team to influence whether
the factory workers team productivity and performance standards level of those wire assemblies of products quality, such as Bill, factory supervisor informed to those factory workers team to increase to produce eight wire

assemblies of numbers one hour for normal three wire assemblies of numbers one hour suddenly. It was caused these workers felt anxious whether who should be dismissed if who could not attempt to produce eight wire assemblies of numbers one hour from Bill, factory supervisor demand. It seemed that the factory workers team norms and goals were not compatible with this company

organizational objectives because this company organizational objective was needed workers finished to produce three wire assemblies of numbers to deliver to every client before schedule

due date. It was depended on the situation of the factory whether it had enough time and machine and skilful worker numbers to supply to finish the identified wire assemblies of numbers to every client identified schedule individually. Otherwise, currently, on this situation, it seemed that

this factory lacked enough worker and machine numbers and enough time and training to those old( current workers), it caused who felt difficult that every worker needed to finish to produce eight wire eight assemblies of numbers minimum per hour to meet this Pacific electronic company client's identified schedule change suddenly.

It also seemed that this company current organizational objective was not same to its prior ( past)

organizational objective, such as every team worker needed to finish to produce three wire assemblies of numbers minimum per hour before to meet this Pacific electronic company client's

identified schedule change suddenly. It was given more difficult to let this factory team every worker to attempt to finish to produce eight wire assemblies of numbers minimum per hour

to meet this current Pacific electronic company client's sudden schedule change. Hence, in this situation, I should feel this factory team norms and goals were not compatible with their company's past organizational objective for this Pacific electronic company's earliest past three wire assemblies of numbers of every worker individual production demand

in the identified schedule. In this situation, this Pacific electronic company client's wire assemblies of production numbers needed to be changed which caused this company factory team expectation schedule and wire assemblies

of production numbers, such as every worker needed to produce eight wire assemblies minimum per hour of numbers of it's production goals and should be changed, but this factory team norms and production goals was still same to this Pacific electronic company client's earliest production numbers, such as every worker needed to produce three wire assemblies of numbers per hour. It meant that who needed have more time and worker and machine numbers to assist them to finish to produce if some workers had no enough effort to produce eight assemblies of numbers per hour to finish to meet this client's identified schedule change, otherwise, who needed to extend time to finish this client's production numbers schedule if none of them could produce eight wire assemblies of numbers at minimum one hour.

This, this factory team norms and goals
seemed that who were not compatible with organizational client's current objective to every worker needed to increase to produce eight wire assemblies of numbers per hour to finish to meet this Pacific electronic company client prior ( not changed) schedule possible. Otherwise, these current factory workers could increase to finish eight wire assemblies of numbers to meet this client's current schedule goals. If this factory team some workers could finish eight or even more wire assemblies of numbers of numbers per hour individually. Thus, this team productivity could still achieve this client's expectation goals to finish to meet on or before schedule. It implied that this team norms and goals was compatible with organizational current objective due to client's expectation wire assemblies of overall increasing numbers had been finished to meet schedule from this factory team overall productivity together. Thus, it caused why this factory team norms and goals would be compatible with organizational team objective of finishing enough wire assemblies of overall numbers to meet this client's schedule date goals possibly or this factory team norms and goals would not be compatible with organization team objective of not finishing enough wire assemblies of overall numbers to meet this client's schedule date goals possibly.

How does the team function to meet individual needs if thsi team factory workers can feel time pressure is reduced to work ?

This company, Steve and Jack were electronic wire assemblies products factory manufactory workers ( members) among of this factory team, who had worked in this factory team five years. Bill was this company factory supervisor, who needed to supervise this workers team to help every business client to finish every electronic wire assemblies of products order to meet whose identified schedule, then delivered to them by shipping channel. Hence, if Bill, factory supervisor who could not lead whose workers team to co-operate to produce the identified electronic wire assemblies of products of numbers to finish to meet the individual business client's identified schedule before due date to deliver to them by shipping. It would cause that this company and the

and the client would feel this company Mr Martin, office manager and Dave, shop of supervisor could not achieve their service agreement to finish electronic wire assemblies identifies numbers to deliver to them before schedule due date. The result would cause this company lost this client, even this company would accept guilty from this client's complaint. Hence, Bill, factory supervisor needed to lead whose workers team to work efficiently to achieve whose job responsibility to finish every individual business client identified good quality and non damaged of electronic wire assemblies of products of numbers to deliver to them by shipping before schedule due date.

In fact, this factory workers team was combined ( co-operated) by every individual worker. Hence, if Bill, factory supervisor expected whose factory team could have good productivity and efficiency, who must individual needs. Otherwise, if some workers did not like to work hard, who would cause this team to delay to finish the identified electronic wire assemblies of numbers to deliver to the individual business client before the schedule due date. Hence, if ill, factory supervisor could satisfy every individual worker needs, then Bill could lead this team to perform more effectively and efficiently. If this factory work could be done by individual without any need for teamwork was not necessary in this factory. I supposed that this factory needed different workers worked in different steps to cooperate to finish every electronic wire assembly product. The reason was possible that because the employer felt every worker could be more proficient to practise to finish the identified step to co-operate to work together in one team, thus every worker could be raised productivity and efficiency in team, it could get more benefits than individual worker did all steps to finish every electronic wire assembly product alone in this factory. However, as the number of this factory team workers increased, the need for cooperation also increased.

As some point, the effort of Bill, factory supervisor who managed the factory team who would outweigh the benefit of having more workers and this factory team performance would began to decline. Hence, if this factory team of worker numbers increased suddenly. Although, every business client's electronic wire assemblies of products individual order finishing time would be reduced possibly, but it seemed that Bill, factory supervisor would feel more difficult to spend more time to lead this team to manage every individual worker who how to co-operate to work more efficiency and who should also feel difficult to satisfy individual worker needs if this team increased many worker numbers sudden seriously. Hence, this factory team overall performance of efficiency and effectiveness would begin to decline for long term due to this factory team increased many worker numbers suddenly to cause every individual worker felt that who could not satisfy more needs than before. Team structure means of coordinating formal team efforts. Leaders are appointed and work rules and procedures are detailed and job descriptions specify individual task responsibilities. It is necessary to coordinate the efforts of individuals assigned to the different tasks. Otherwise, tasks may not be performed in the correct sequence and employees may duplicate their efforts or work against each other. It seemed that this factory workers team which electronic wire assembling steps could be similar to bank loan department and collection department steps. If one individual worker who had much effort to finish whose wire assembling job step more quick to compare another less effort worker individual wire assembling job step. It seemed that the much effort worker could have much time to attempt to help the another less effort worker to finish whose step. Hence, it was possible that this factory team function could compare every individual worker's effort whether who could had more effort and time to help other worker to finish whose wire assembly job step during the less effort worker could not finish whose wire assembling step quickly.Thus, this factory team function could evaluate whether who individual worker had more effort and much time to attempt to help another less effort individual worker to finish their wire assembling job step for every individual client. It implied that these much effort individual workers who had needs to pay to optimal compensation more than the less effort individual workers for whose better performance in the factory team.

It was possible that the piece pay rate compensation was not suitable to these more effort individual worker to satisfy whose individual needs to accept in the team because who could increase return to multi tasking, in which the same workers did both easy to observe tasks, such as wire assembling production of every step and hard to observe tasks, such as process improvement of wire assembling production of every step and producing exact wire assembling quantities of output ( no more and no less). I suggest this factory ought change piece rate compensation to time rate compensation and gain sharing payment method to the more effort individual worker productivity , the individual more effort worker who could receive time rate compensation plus a usually small amount bonus linked to the productivity of the establishment to this factory team during who could increase

return to multi tasking to assist whom to finish the another job step of less effort worker's wire assembling job duty for any individual client's wire assembling products delivering order before schedule due date. I supposed that this factory team function adopted transfer lines in which individual worker was

transferred between stations either by machines or by a moving conveyor assembly line. In either case, time rates compensation were more advantages than piece rates compensation due to

it was more fair to the every more effort individual worker if who could finish whose wire assembling individual step before schedule due date and who had more time to assist another

less effort worker to help who to finish whose wire assembly step immediately. In result, these every individual workers could raise this team efficiency to help this factory team to finish the identified wire assembly numbers to deliver to any client by shipping before the schedule due date normally.

Bill, factory supervisor and Dave shop of supervisor who both could obtain high effort from this factory workers on observable tasks by noticing where the wire assembly inventory piles up between stations, without incurring the costs of piece rates. I supposed that the wire assembling products required operations on different machines, performed in different orders setting up fixed paths for work to travel would have made low effort in production more observable, but would have made the wire assembling production process very inflexible. Therefore, Bill, factory supervisor needed put each individual worker in charge of a machine that could do several jobs. ( each with a negotiated rat) and encouraged this team workers to do each job quickly via piece rates. Since there was recurring demand for each wire assembling product for a long time, management did not have to negotiate new piece rates very often. I suggested that Bill, factory supervisor should design the observable tasks , e.g. the step of wire assembling production to be done by one group of factory workers and the unobservable making improvement to the step of wire assembling production, fixing problems to be done by another group with a different compensation scheme and observable and unobservable tasks were separated in this factory team.

Thus, wire assembly production workers focused on producing output and were paid to piece rate. Quality was the responsibility of other departments workers, such as inspectors, who identified defective parts and engineers , who attempted to design less defect wire assembly products and processes, these all individual workers who every was paid time rates. All else equal, the low rates compensation was paid to less effort individual worker per piece and the higher rates and bonus compensation was paid to high effort individual worker per time rate to finish every individual business client's order. Finally, this factory team function could give synergy to achieve an effect of the total output of this factory team is greater than the combined outputs of individual worker working alone.

In conclusion, this factory team function could use time rates and bonus compensation method to pay to the individual more effort every worker to let who to feel this employer was more fair to every individual worker performance. The more effort workers ought have more reasonable compensation to compare the less effort workers in this factory team.

If I was Dave, shop supervisor, what team concepts should I apply to achieve time pressure reducing aim to let these factory electronic workers to feel? why?

If I was Dave, shop supervisor, I should apply these team concepts to this electronic factory wire assembling team. When, managers assign associates to teams, who often make three common assumptions, which can lead to mistakes; such as, who assume that a large team size always better and who assume that everyone knows how or is suited to work in a team and who assume that people who are similar to each other will work better together and so they can co-operate happily. Group means two or more interdependent individuals who influence one another through social interaction. Thus, if I was Dave, shop supervisor, I and my shop staffs would be one group. Bill,
factory supervisor and factory team workers who would be another group factory workers team ; Mr Martin, office manager and office staffs would be another group top managers team.

Our company needed these three groups communicate and co-operate to work together to deliver message between about of us about every individual business client's wire assembly product numbers demand and schedule due date to ensure when every client's order could confirm to finish to deliver to the client by shipping factory supervisor and whose workers was a team because this team had two or more workers with work roles that required them to be interdependent who operated within a large social system, as our factory performing tasks, such as every individual worker needed to produce every part of wire assembling in different stage relevant to our organization's mission , such as finishing the indicated wire assembling numbers to meet individual client's schedule to deliver to whom by shipping with consequences that affected others inside, such as Bill, factory supervisor and others outside, such as Dave, shop supervisor and Mr Martin , office manager of our organization, such as company and Bill, factory supervisor had membership that was identified to these on factory team and those not on the team, such as Dave, shop supervisor and sellers teams as well as Mr Martin, office manager and office administration teams. Effective team performance can be more difficult to achieve when team members belong to difficult identify groups or when their identification with these groups conflicts with the goals and objectives of the team, such as these factory some workers who felt difficult to raise to produce eight wire assembling from these wire assemblies in this factory team, but Mr Martin, office manager needed Dave, shop supervisor to notify to Bill, factory supervisor to let whose factory workers every one to know whether who could raise productivity to this

eight numbers and who could not, then who decided whether how to solve that Pacific electronic company client could not receive wire assemblies of identified number before schedule due date by shipping.

In fact, Dan shop supervisor would had conflict, with Mr Martin, office manager who explained

workers felt wages were less, so who would not worked hard to raise effort to produce more wire assemblies, but Mr Martin , office manager disagreed whose suggestion and who enforced Dan, factory supervisor to enquire whether these factory workers who could do eight wire assemblies possibly, it would cause some workers felt anxious to be dismiss if who could not finish this numbers. This, these group conflicts caused non effective team performance with the factory group goals

and the shop group goals and management group goals which were more different. If I was Dave, shop supervisor of this electronic company, I would apply management team

concept to my shop group because I believed we were both the senior level

shop manager and office manager who needed to coordinate the activities of our respective units, e.g. shop top management teams and office top management teams as well as Mr Martin, office management group . Otherwise, Bill, factory supervisor would be production team because workers who needed to supervise whose factory workers group to produce tangible products, such as identified wire assemblies
of numbers to meet every individual client's schedule due date.
A final consideration in Dave, shop supervising team effectiveness is whether a supervising team is needed to perform the work at all or whether the work is best performed by Dave,
shop supervisor individually.

In this case, it would have been better to have individual separately, Dave, shop supervising team effectiveness is measured on knowledge criteria, affective criteria and outcome criteria. Knowledge criteria reflected the degree to which Dave, shop supervisor individually increased its performance capability . Affective criteria addressed the question of whether Dave, shop supervisor individually
had a fulfilling and satisfying to supervise shop experience, such as whether Dan could manage whose shop and factory effectively. Outcome criteria referred to Dan 's personal quality of the shop supervisor how to supervise whose shop and factory teams effectively. Hence, if I was Dan this electronic company shop supervisor, I shall apply these team concepts to apply to whose shop and factory teams management in this situation.

# CHAPTER FOUR

# Developing country labors abnormal long time working hours influences

This research is about Hong Kong employers need labors to work abnormal long time working hours whether it can assist Hong Kong economic growth and raise productivity both in the long term.

The outcome is either Hong Kong labors work long time working hours abnormally who can not rise Hong Kong economic growth or who can rise Hong Kong economic growth in long time. Generally, Hong Kong employers choose to pay less salary expenditure to need many extra labors to work abnormal working hours to help them to rise productivity, but who don't concern that long time working factor will influence unhealthy to current workers due to who need to work long time working hours abnormally in long time and it seems to cause their workers will reduce productivity and inefficiency in long time.

Although, it is possible that HK labors can be increased extra abnormal working hours to work to rise Hong Kong employers' productivity and assist HK social economy will be grown up in short term, but it is also possible that it can't rise Hong Kong economic growth due to their unhealthy or sick increasing to cause productivity declining and inefficiency in long time. Thus, I shall find evidence to analyze whether Hong kong labors need to work abnormal long time working hours. Otherwise, who will decline Hong Kong economic growth and reduce productivity and inefficiency in long time as well as I shall give suggestion to indicate whether either current workers work abnormal long time working hours or employers ought choose to employ more extra part time workers to assist current labors to rise their productivity to decide which is the best choice to raise HK economic growth and efficient productivity in long time.

1.1 What is abnormal working hours Economic Problem

Effects on Hong Kong employment of working time reduction is found to be difficult to predict. The results of Hong Kong macroeconomic simulations of the effects on employments of working time reduction rely heavily on certain basic assumptions, such as how many hours people will actually work or how productivity and pay levels will develop. Whether HK abnormal working hours will assist HK social economic growth or economic falling down in long term.

The reasons cause Hong Kong labours who need to work abnormal long time working hours. In fact, it isn't the reason that the Hong Kong high skilful labours market is shortage to supply for the nature of some occupations, e.g. hospital doctors and nurses, university teachers, law firm lawyers etc professional occupations. Hk has many high qualification university students graduation, it has enough labor supply to high labor market evey year. The reason is that employers don't like to spend more salary to increase to employ extra labors to share current workers workload, such as low skilful and hardworking labors, such as cleaners, securities, waiters and high skilful professionals, such as hospital doctors and nurses, university teachers, lawyers etc. However, the low and high skilful labor market can be enough supply in Hong Kong, but Hong Kong employers need the current high and low both skilful workers who need to work more than 10 to 12 hours or more per working day commonly. It is possible that HK high and low educational labours will be caused unhealthy and lack enough sleep if who still need to work abnormal working hours time in long time. Although, who can rise productivity and efficiency in the short time, but it is possible that who can't rise productivity and inefficiency in the long time. Moreover, it will cause many young or middle or old ages high educational or low educational knowledgeable hardworking workers who will lose many jobs provided and who will be hard to find any jobs in HK labor employment market if HK employers don't choose to pay extra salaries to employ extra full time workers to share current labors' workload in the high and low salary occupations, due to they only choose to increase abnormal additional extra working hours to current workers to achieve to reduce employment expenditure and raise productivity. Hence, it is possible to influence HK social economy grows up slowly, even it's economy can go down seriously in long time.

Hypotheses Testing And Data Analysis

I shall assume that working wage or salary of every individual labors can not be increased, even can be decreased as well as whose normal working hours can be increased abnormally in generally. This means that the Hong Kong individual worker's income will be decreased and general productivity raising is not affected generally, due to HK employers need current labors to work abnormal extra working hours to attempt to raise productivity daily, but their salary or wage have not increased more. However, HK employers need many workers to accomplish the same amount of work, even who don't like to employ extra labors to assist current workers to achieve long term productivity rasing in their companies. These abnormal working hours labors will feel unfair treatment, due to they need to work abnormal working hours, but their salary or wage have not been increased. In the first scenario of my hypothesis is about that HK labor employment market's general salary or wage has not been increased to the normal proportion of the increased extra abnomal working time(hours). Then, in HK labors market, due to the numbers of labors supply is more than the jobs supply because HK employers don't like to pay more salary or wage expenditure to employ extra labor, but they like to increase extra abnormal working hours to current workers to aim to achieve productivity. So it will cause many HK job seekers with adequate qualifications or with less qualifications who won't find any jobs easily, then the HK the numbers of unemployed people will be increased and their household incomes will decrease to cause many HK household do not like to spend easily. The result will cause a negative effect on HK social private consumption will be decreased and the businessmen' income will be decreased also. So, HK people private consumption decreasing will influence HK economy growth to be slow, even it will cause HK economy declining in the long time.

In the second scenario of my hypothesis is about that Hong Kong workers are fully compensated for the increasing extra abnormal working time(hours) by the abnormal additional working hours calculation. Although, Hong Kong companies' productivity will be raised, but which are not to the extent that it compensates Hong Kong enterprises for their increased wage or salary costs. In fact, Hong Kong enterprises, their costs are passed on to the clients, it causes Hong Kong's economic growth has an impact on international competitiveness to cause economic declining in possible when these enterprises need to raise their products' sale prices to balance their salary or wage cost rasing to win their import competitors. Another effect is that Hong Kong individual labor's incomes decrease, which means that Hong Kong private consumption also falls in this scenario to influence HK economic growth seriously. Thus, the HK economic growth problem will be caused, due to these factors lead to a fall in Hong Kong social household private consumption. Consequently, it will cause many HK employers hope to raise Hong Kong productivity and they will raise the total amount of Hong Kong labor actually worked hours will be risen to such as extent as the increasing in normal working time(hours) from 8 or 9 hours per normal working day to 10 or 11 or 12 hours, even more extra abnormal hours per working day to the current labors. But they do not like to spend more salary or wage expenditure to employ full time extra labors, instead of increasing extra abnormal working hours to current labors to achieve productivity of raising, due to the cost will be increased if they choose to employ extra full time labors if they want to raise productivity. However, I feel they will raise productivity in the short term, but they will not raise productivity in the long term when they choose to raise their current labors abnormal working hours per working day.

The assumption will be made regarding to the relationship between the HK labor market's abnormal long time working hours factor and whether it can influence Hong Kong economic growth in long time for this research economic problem. For example, how many hours Hong Kong labor would actually work or how much workers have efficient productivity and efficiency and how much salaries or wages would be affected as a result of the increasing in working time(hours) in Hong Kong employment market.

I shall apply endogenous growth theory to Hong Kong labor market. As this theory indicates that this model also incorporated a new concept of human capital, whose capital is increasing rates of return. Research done in this area has focused on what increases human capital ( e.g. education) or technological change ( e.g. innovation) to influence HK economic growth. In macro economic environment, it indicates that economic growth means the increase in the market value of the products and services produced by the country's economy over time. It is conventionally measured as the percent rate of increase in real growth domestic product or real GDP. The growth of the ratio of GDP to population (GDP per capital, per capita income). Thus, an increase in growth is caused by more efficient use of inputs is referred to as intensive growth. GDP growth is caused only be increased in such as capital, population or territory is called extensive growth. Thus, in economy growth theory, typically refers growth off potential output, i.e. production is at full employment. However, HK unemployment ratio is still high to compare other developed or developing countries, although the labors supply are enough to HK employment market.

The working time is the period of time that an individual spends at paid occupation labor. Many countries regulate the work week by law, such as minimum daily rest periods, annual holidays and a maximum number of working hours per week. Working time may vary from person to person often depending on location, cultural, lifestyle choice and the profitability of the individual's livelihood.

Generally, most Hong Kong employers need labours work long time working hours abnormally. For example, low educational workers, such as security occupations of labors need to work per working day is twelve hours or more, restaurant waiters and dish cleaners also need to work ten to twelve hours or more per working day, bank counter cashiers or audit firm staffs also need to work over time from 10 to 12 hours or more per working day and who have no extra salaries for over time salaries payment commonly. Standard working hours or normal working hours refers to the legislation to limit the working hours per day, per week, per month or per year. If an employee needs to work overtime, the employer will need to pay overtime payments to employees as required in the law. Generally speaking, standard working hours countries wordwide are around 40 to 44 hours per week (but not everywhere: such as France employers need labors work from 35 hours per week, North Korea employers need labors work up to 112 hours per week). Maximum working hours refers that the employee can't work than the level specified in the maximum working hours law. It seems that Hong Kong many employers had needed labors to work above standard working hours per week to compare to other developed countries, e.g. America, France, England, New Zealand etc. developed countries.

On the 20th century, work hours are declined by almost half, mostly due to rising wages are brought about by renewed economic growth with a supporting role from legislation human rights. The decline countined at a faster in Europe: For example, France adopted a 35 hours work week in 2000 year. In 1995, China adopted a 40 hours week, eliminating half day work on Saturday. Technology has also continued to improve worker productivity, permitting standards of living to rise as hours declined. In developed economies, as the time needed to manufacturing products has declined more working hours have become available to provide services. In fact, on the one hand, Hong Kong manufacturing industry has declined, such as clothing, shoes, toy etc. manufacturing industry. On the other hand, its service industry need many labors to supply in the labor market per day, e.g. banking, accounting, restaurant, security etc. service sectors. A reduction in Hong Kong working time can be accomplished in various ways, and that Hong Kong enterprise's production costs will be affected in different ways depending on what type of measured is used. Usually Hong Kong employers would be likely to ask those already employed to do more overtime or who will require part time workers to increase whose working hours, especially would pass salaries expense from them on to charge higher sale price to their clients. Then, which would increase the rate of inflation and weaken competitiveness to win overseas competitors' product import.

I shall use these methods to examine this research problem, e.g. statistical analysis and economic concepts, such as GDP, economic growth and labor participation rate. Aim to research whether HK abnormal long time working hours can raise productivity and influence HK economic growth in long term. As regards Hong Kong enterprises' productivity, my research will be discussed what factors that may lead to either an increase or a decrease in productivity and I shall conclude what the effects are very difficult to assess as conditions vary between and it will concern within different service industry sectors, e.g. hotel, bank, restaurant, security, professional service etc. service occupations. These service labors of numbers are more than manufacture labors of numbers in Hong Kong nowadays. Of vital importance for the effect on Hong Kong employment of a reduction of working time is the extent to which wages or salaries are adopted. If the occupations where there was a shortage of labors, Hong Kong employers were to try to contibute to higher pay claims to long time working labors. According to the 1961 year population census, the size of the economically active population was approximately 1.2 million during that year and who was also economically active population was seeking worker. The labor force had grown to 3.1 million by 1996 year ( William. C & Wing. S, 1997).

In 1996 year, HK economy was industrialization process filled by a large supply of relativey unskilled but hardworking labor, many of them were refugees from China, the dominance of manufacturing has been largely displaced by commerce and service sector and the demand for unskilled labor is falling relative to the demand for skilled and educated workers in Hong Kong. According to the 1961 year population census, the size of the economically active population was approximately 1.2 million during that year and who was also economically active population or the active seeking worker. The labor force had grown to 3.1 million by 1996 year ( William. C & Wing. S, 1997). William. C & Wing. S (1997) also indicated that HK Census and Statistics department ( various years) reported specific labor participation rate and size of the Hong Kong force from 1961 year to 1996 year. "During this period the size of the labor force grew from 1.2 million to 2.5 million. The annual rate of increase was 3.7%. It implies labor supply increased so rapidly, so labor intensive industries were developed. However, Hong kong population had increased to 7 million till to 2015 year." Hence the size of the labor force had increased more and it implied labors would supply more than employers demand. But, HK employer job supply numbers are less than HK labor demand numbers in HK employment market. It seems that if HK employers did not like to spend more salaries expenditure to employ extra labors to rise productivity, it would cause many young single or married people unemployed.

Any countrie's economic growth are usually calculated in real terms. i.e. inflation adjusted terms to eliminate the effect of inflation on the price of products produced. Economic growth has the indirect potential to reduce poverty, as a result of an increase in employment opportunities and increased labor productivity. However, employment is no guarantee of escaping poverty. The international labor organization estimates that is as many as 40% of workers are poor, not earning enough to keep families above the $2 a day poverty line. For instance, in India, poor are wage earner in formal employment because jobs are insecure and low paid and offer no chance to accumulate wealth to avoid risk, other countries found bigger benefits from focusing more no productivity improvement than low skilled work. Thus, increase in employment without increase in productivity lead to rise in the number of working poor and these countries don't apply the creation of quality and not quantity in labor market policies. In Vietnam, for example, employment growth has slowed when productivity growth has continued. Furthermore, productivity increases don't always lead to increase wages, e.g. United States, the gap between productivity and wages was been rising since the 1980 year. The overseas Development Institute study showed that other sectors were just as important in reducing unemployment as manufacturing.

Nowadays, the services sector is most effective as translating productivity growth into employment growth in Hong Kong. The HK Government forecast (2012) indicated that "HK's economy has slowed, growing by 0.9% year-on year in the half of 2012 year, after expanding by 5% in 2011 year. For 2012 year, the economy is forecast to grow at 1-2%. Consumer prices increased by 5.3% in 2011 year and 4.7% year-on-year in the first half of 2012 year. The unemployment rate was 3.2% for April-June 2012 year, compared with 3.4% for 2011 year." Although, it seemed that unemployment rate decreased 0.2% for April to June 2012, but its unemployment was still existed. Moreover, HK's economy has slowed to grow by 0.9% only year-on-year in the first half of 2012 year and HK government forcast to grow at 1-2% for 2012. By United States Government statistic in 2006 year, the average man employed full time worked 8.4 hours mandatory minimum amount of paid time off for sickness or holiday. However, regular full time workers often have the opportunity to take about nine days off for various holiday. However, regular full time workers of skill leave and two weeks ( 10 business days) of paid holiday time with some workers receiving additional time after several years. Because of the pressure of working time with some workers receiving additional time after several years. It seems United States developed countries some workers still feel pressure of working shorten working hours can reduce the pressure of working. In fact, HK many professional workers put in longer hours than the forty hour standard per week. A forty hours work week is considered inadequate and may result in job loss or failure to be promoted. Although, these employers don't spend much salary expenditures to employ extra professional workers to share whose workload and who can perform to serve whose clients efficiently in the short time. But in the long time, it is possible that who will work pressure possibly due to who need to serve many clients every day, and whose working performance will become to be poor to cause inefficiently. Until now, HK has no legislations regarding maximum and normal working hours. The average weekly working hours of full time employees in HK is 49 hours. According to the Price and Earnings report (2012) conducted by UBS, when the global and regional average were 1,915 and 2,154 hours per year respectively, the average working hours in HK is 2,296 hours per year, which ranked the fifth longest yearly working hours among 72 countries under study. In addition, the survey is conducted by the public opinion study group of the University of HK, it showed 79% of the respondents agree that the problem of overtime work in HK is "serve" and 65% of the respondents agree that the legislation on the maximum working hours. In HK, 70% of surveyed don't receive any overtime remuneration. These show that people in HK concerns the working time issues. The equilibrium price for a certain types of labor is the wage rate. The model of labor market, even given all its assumption is logically. The criticism of application of the model of supply and demand generalizes particularly to all markets for factor of production, e.g. labor working hours. I assume HK employers don't like to employ many labors to assist current labors to raise service or productivity when their client numbers have increased. It is possible that who feel salaries expenditure can not be exceed to their reasonable budget. Hence, who need current labors to work long time hours to do too much work, even the HK labor supply is increasing and it will cause many people lose jobs. It seems HK service industry can influence its economic growth. If those service industry labors need to work long time, who will feel mental pressure to work unhealthly and who need have enough sleep. If who can't have enough sleep to face every day work in long term, whose working performance will be poor or reduce productivity to whose clients possibly in long time. I believe HK service industry labors work long time working hours per week that it will influence whose service performance to be poor. In fact, most developed countries labors working hours are less than HK seriously. For example, United States originating from the traditional American business hours of 9:00 AM to 5:00 PM. Monday to Friday, representing a workweek of five to eight hour per working day composing 40 hours in total. The actual time at work often varies between 35 and 48 hours in practice due to breakers. In many traditonal white collar positions, employees were required to be in the office during these hours to take orders from the bosses, workplace hours have become more flexible. Another example, South Korea has the fastest declining working time, which is the result of proactive more to lower working hours at all levels to increase leisure and than the 10 days of the united States and double that of the England's 8 days. Also, work hours in and 40 hour week ( 44 hours in specified workplaces). The overtime limits are: 15 hours a week, allowance should not be lower than 125% and not more than 150% of normal hourly rate. However, Hong Kong dish cleaners, bank cashiers occupations whose need to work over time often , due to client numbers are increasing every days and their employers do not plan to employ extra workers to share their work loading. Hence, it seems whose work over time are similar to work abnormal long time working hours in every week in HK.

Middison A.(2001) indicated that "the unemployment rate is a performance indicator of the economy." The purpose of economic activity is to transform productive resources into products and services. An economy that uses all or most of its labor force should clearly be considered as a better performing economy than one that lacks the ability to put all or most of its labor force into work and thus some labor productive respurces can not be used. In fact, in economy theory, labor demand is considered to be a derived demand, meaning that its demand is explained not by itself, but by the existence of demand for products and services that use labor as a factor production. If labor demand is a desired demand, then an assessment of the performance of the economy could certainly profit from an evaluation of how well a specific social system managers to transform labor input into products and services. It is convenient to distinguish between economic performance of an economic system and labor market performance. The former related with the ability of a social system to deliver products and services and the latter related with the important, but more specific issue, of how well the labor market managers to match supply and demand. Economic and Trade Information on HK (2012) key indicators of the labor market had finished sample simple average of 15 countries statistic analysis to show "the result was as for the role of work hours in explaining GDP per capital had negative relation between GDP and working hours, as if long working hours where used to compensate the low productivity. The historical downward trend of working time form the slightly less than 3000 annual hours per person employed of the 1870 year to the less than 1600 year of the late 1990 year could be taken as a confirmation of this hypothesis." Thus, this hypothesis could be supported by viewpoint. It was about HK long time working hours ought not increase HK GDP and long working hours where used to compensate the low productivity to HK employers in the long time.

What is difference benefits between normal working hours
and abnormal working hours

These research will have these two questions to be answer:
1. Can Hong Kong this individual labour abnormal long time working hours factor gives welfare benefit to every labor in the long time?
2. Can Hong Kong this abnormal labor working hours factor grow HK

society whole economy in the long time?

It seems that HK employers don't like to employ extra workers to share current worker's workload, even the supply of labours is enough. Due to who do not want to pay extra each worker's salaries to raise whose productivity. To explain relationship between the workers abnormal long time working hours factor and the other resources input factor to influence HK enterprises growth in an improved model in the long time. I shall develop a model is the selection of two variables to explore. These variables have a cause and effect relationship. I shall suppose HK employers believe that workers abnormal long time working hours which can raise their productivity efficiently and which can assist HK society overall economic growth in the long time. These variables have a cause and effect relationship. From this discussion to investigate HK society overall economic growth effect is caused by companies' variable factors. The variable factors include the raising of abnormal long time working hours factor or increasing capital and machinery and equipment and building assets factor or raising natural resources for production factor or taking risking of success or failure ability in an productive enterprise factor. Thus, these separate sets of variable have been indentifies and each set could be selected for a model. In fact, Hong Kong society overall economic growth disputes many occur because a variety of resources input factors can be considered to analyze an effect cause whether which kind of resources input factors which can cause HK society economy growth is fast or slow. In my viewpoint, my exploring reasons are for a slow growing economy in HK. Some economists focus on relationship between money supply and growth in society, some in society's spending growth and some on the price level. In fact, HK economic growth is slow in the long time. I shall focus on the relationship between the HK companies' workers abnormal long time working hours factor and the other resources input factor both to influence HK society overall economic growth. Hence, I shall give assupmtions and conditions are held to be true when exploring the relationship is between HK companies and resources input variables within a model. For example, the relationship is between HK economic growth is slow or fast and labor resources supply numbers are not shortage. But HK employers ususally employ their limited numbers of labors to cause current workers need to overtime work or work in abnormal long time working hours often. Understanding the factors behind labor participation decision is an important component of the understanding long time change in labor supply in Hong Kong society.

In my another viewpoint, discussing HK labor supply, it is important to distinguish between the supply economy. The supply of Hong Kong labor to particular firm, an industry can be highly responsive to wages or salaries as workers seek the most profitable employment in HK. The supply of labors to HK society economy. On the other hand, it is typically less elastic to the labors who often change new jobs because most HK employers who need workers who work long time working hours to cause most HK labors can't have much chance to change new jobs which can provide normal working hours. So, it seems that who won't choose to change new jobs often because many HK employers who need HK labors work abnormal working hours nowadays.

HK employees of large companies of public utilities sector and the HK Government both organizations which typically enjoy more benefits and have greater job security than employers of small firms in Hong Kong society. This has lead to cause a distinction between the small HK private companies and public HK Government and public utilities sector. In fact, nowadays, most HK jobs have changes to service job nature from manufacturing job nature. However, deregulation, downsizing and pressure factors have caused many HK large companies which choose change working hours from normal 7 to 8 hours per working day to adnormal 9 to 12 hours or more per working day. Specically, the occupations of service sector job nature include: restaurant waitors, banking counter servicers, professional lawyers, share agents, security servicers, accountants etc. different service sector occupation labors. The result will cause the labors who choose to leave whose employers if who could not accept to work abnormal working hours to their current employers. Even, it will also cause the current workers who feel nervous and tired and worry to work in pressure everyday, due to who need to increase many extra hours to work often and who will lose their private entertainment time with their family or friends often, even it will be unhealthy to them due to who lack sleeping. Although, HK business cycle was the short term economy in manufacturing macroeconomic environment in beginning from 1950 year. Then, HK economy growth had developed, so many the demanding of labor numbers had been caused to increase seriously till to nowadays. The economic and trade information on Hong Kong of HK Government statistic department (2012) reported " the HK economy was forecasted to grow at 1-2% for 2012 year and it's economy had slowed growing by 0.9% per year in the half of 2012 year after expanding by 5% in 2011 year." Although, it implied that HK labor market had enough labor numbers supply. Otherwise, many HK employers don't like to employ many labor numbers to share current workers' workload. It is possible that due to whose HK current workers need to spend adnormal working hours to raise their productivity per working day to save spending extra salaries or wages expenditures to pay to employ extra labors in HK current labor market. I feel that HK economy growth is slow or poor because the main reason is due to HK Government doesn't spend expenditures to assist HK employers to raise training to their current HK labors to provide human capital to achieve to raise whose service performance to improve their efficient productivity in HK service businesses sector only in the long time. Finally, the results were discovered and will be backed by these evidences.

Can abnormal working hours raise productivity and economic growth in long term

My essay will truly be a qualitative and quantitative research, it is based on experimental fact and evidence. To research the long time employment influence relationship is between the labor abnormal long time working hours factor and the influence of HK economic growth in productive model factor both. This study suggests understanding of the relationship between economic growth influences and HK labors abnormal working hours need to be raised. In fact, the HK labor force participation rate will be fallen every year. Economic growth in HK was through phases that affects growth through changes in the labor force participation rate and the relative sizes of HK society service and manufacturing sectors. In fact, HK agricultural industry sector is not existed and manufacturing industry sector numbers are decreasing and it begins to enter service industry sector. The low knowledge level of jobs include security, banking, restaurant, cleaning, transportation etc. service nature of jobs as well as the high knowledge level of jobs include lawyer, accountant, medicine, doctor, computer technician etc. professonal service nature of jobs which both are providing service to HK society nowadays. The investment theory indicates that the education is as investment human capital to provide to any companies. The main difference is that human capital is incorporated in human beings and it can't be resold. When physical capital can be acquired at almost any desired amount in boom periods and be resold during recession on secondary markets, human capital can be acquired mostly in the beginning of individual behavior by firms. I shall recommend HK companies ought choose these methods to control labors whose working hours time efficiently.

Yasuhiro (2014) showed that "wage differentials based on age and length of service in-house training refers to a process whereby workers acquire skills through daily work and occasional of the job training. Whether or not they perceive it as "training" is irrelevant. Training is also included informal learning conducted independently by the worker without any feedback from an instructor. Conceptually, the skills acquired are divided into general skills that can be used in the company currently employing the worker. The process of acquiring the latter specific training." Generally, when companies minimizes personnel costs, the ratio of marginal productivity referred to below as productivity between workers are equal to wage ratios. Therefore, the coefficient of age in the wage function expresses the rate of productivity increases due to general training and the coefficient of length of service and the rate of wage increases due to special training reason. The sum of both coefficients will express the rate of productivity increase in current companies due to training is as an important causing factor.

In conclusion, in my viewpoint, HK employers need to provide on job training to current labors to aim to raise their efficiency to productivity in the long time. Because when their labors had been trained to let them to learn how to use special skill to finish their job duties easily, then they will not need to spend much time ( additional working hours ) to finish their job duties per working day. On the one hand, HK employers need to measure to compare what benefits are in favour of standard working hours to whose employees. The benefits include, such as promoting work life balance and enjoy family life, increasing time for leisure and rest, beneficial to health and employees can have more time to pursue further studies as well as employers do not need to pay higher salaries to longer working hours employees or overtime pay boost income as most HK companies pay time and a half to some employees only. On the other hand, HK employers need to measure to compare what benefits are against standard working hours to employers, such as employing many part time working hours employees to assist normal working hours full time employees rather than needing full time employees work abnormal hours daily, lowering or cancelling year and bonuses etc. Moreover, HK employers may also use various measure to offset the increased cost of running businesses, such as lowering average hourly anual compensation. However, when HK employees are forced to work part time jobs, who may need to acquire additional employment to maintain their standard living. Even, HK employers only force employees to work overtime in some situations. Appropriate standard working hours can vary across different industries based on the type of work performed. Such as some HK certain professional positions are difficult to define in terms of appropriate working hours. Issues can arise with employers expecting exployees to work extra hours "off the clock" in order to keep costs down. Thus, I believe that HK labors abnormal working hours time issue ought be decreased and HK employers ought employ extra workers assistance to share current labors' workload to help them to raise productivity and efficiency and HK economy will grow fast in the long time. Finally, my research aims to find that the number of hours worked is a more responsive measure of the state of the labor market than employment in HK. Comparing the number of hours worked to indicators of the wider economy shows that it is likely to be demand from HK firms ( employers) which is driving the numbers of hours, rather than individual job applicant supplys to HK employment market. My analysis also show that the HK appears to have developed a long working hours culture to compare other developed countries, such as America, England, Canada etc. In fact, in the presence of HK firms may even invest to find which are more profitable to able to reduce their every employee's abnormal working hours daily rather than normal number of working hours of their every employee.

Bibliography

Economic And Trade Information On Hong Kong, (14 Aug. 2012). Hong Kong Government Forecast for 2012, retrieved from the following URL: http://www.cepa.hktdc.com

Middison A. (2001). The World Economy. A Millennial Perspective, OECD, Paris.

Yasuhio, U. (2014). Japan Labor Review, vol.11 no.3,

High Economic Growth And Human Capital:

Conditions For Sustained Growth, Konan

University.

William, C&Wing, S.(1997). The Hong Kong Economic

Policy Studies Series, published by City University

Of HK Press, Hong Kong

# Behavioral economy method predicts organizational behavioral changes and marketing behavioral changes

Over the past 20 years, many researchers believe to apply behavioral economic macroeconomic models which can predict market behavioral change. The reasons are based on assumptions of optimizing behavior in many cases have difficulty accounting for key real-world observations. Hence, researchers have used behavioral economics assumptions with the aim of making their model predicting better fit the data. The reason for behavioral economics results into macroeconomics will be more accurate to predict market behavioral change in macro-economy view point, such as economic fluctuation prediction, the consumption, formation of expectations and determination of wages and employment how to aggregation supply and the possibility of consumer individual demand product or service number prediction more accurately.

● How to apply behavioral economy theory to predict marketing behavioral changes more accurate?

Anyway, economists aim to develop models of human behavior and interactions in market in order to build useful models. Economists make simplifying assumptions to analyze why the market will be changed by consumer individual consumption behavior changing.

Why do I assume consumers are as economic man ? In behavioral economy view point, how the perception of the economic man's behavior (including consumer choices) of economic models with the development of economics as a science. Economists explain the concept of economics as a science. It is the concept of consumer as an economic man, the essence and complexity of consumer behavior.

The consumer and consumer purchasing behavior are an important area of interest of many scientific disciplines. The process of economic decision making as well as consumption choices are connected with wider human activities. The terms of both consumer individual attitudes and group social behavior will influence group social behavior will influence consumer individual final consumption decision in every consumption choice process. Thus, behavioral economy method can predict consumer behavioral changing, it can apply these sciences to research, includes sociology, psychology, anthropology, operational research, decision theory etc. different literature research aspects. I assume that businessmen can apply behavioral economy method to predict market changing behaviors successfully if they own behavioral economy knowledge.

In this part, I shall concentrate on explain how the perception of the economic man's behavior ( including consumer choice) is applied to predict market behaviors. After explaining the concept of consumer as an economic man, the nature and complexity of consumer behavior are discussed to below different industries' marketing behavioral changing every case studies in US or UK countries.

Why is consumer as an economic man? IN behavioral economy view point, the concept of answer is one of the fundamental concepts in economics because the consumer is the case market participant along with the producer. In general, lecturers define the consumer in various ways, but in behavioral economy view point, consumers mean economy man. Because who will compare cost and benefit to any product or service to decide to choose to buy the product or consume the service. Consumers are as "economic man", who will make own subjective preferences ( tastes), habits and traditions and existing objective constraints ( i.e. disposal income) market prices of products and services in order to satisfy whose needs to a maximum degree and in the most rational way.

Thus, economic man means consumers need to make psychological mind to decide whether who either prefer to buy this product or another product or prefer to consume this service or another service more suitable. Thus, any markets or industries need have themselves benefits and consumers must need to evaluate whether the product or service has more benefits to compare other products or services in the consumption market to satisfy whose needs. It means that if the product or service has more benefits to compare other similar products or services. Then the product or service will persuade many consumers to choose to but the product or consume the service.

Consequently, in first part, I shall indicate how to apply behavioral economy theory : economic man psychological method, benefits and costs benefits method, how to predict these US and UK enterprises marketing behavioral changing more accurate.

In the second part, I shall apply micro employee behavioral economy concept to explain how to solve these US and UK inter-organizational management challenge.

I believe that behavioral economy method can be applied to research organizational employee behaviors change, e.g. how any why the employee chooses to do this action in whose organization. Moreover, behavioral economy method can be applied to consumption market to predict how any why the consumer choose to buy the product or consume the service. So, any consumers and employees personal psychology and external environment economic factor will influence how to choose to do decision in any organizations or consumption environment.

Bibliography

Bandiera, O., I. Barankay, and I. Rasul ( 2005). Social preferences and the response to incentives: Evidence from personal data. The quarterly journal of economics 120 (3), 917-969.

Exadaktylos, F., A.M. Espin and P. Branas-Garza (2013). Experimental subjects are not different. Scientific reports 3, 1213.

Lazear, E.P. (1979). Why is there mandatory retirement? Journal of political economy 87(6), 1261-1284.

Consumer psychological time method predicts stable basic income consumer individual spending behavior

Can apply consumer psychological time method to predict that the consequences of a stable basic income consumer's consumption behavior? It may be significantly different than the ones are predicted by the standard economic model if more realistic assumptions of human consumption behavioral prediction success.

Consumer psychological time method assumes that consumer will compare whether whose benefits are more than costs after they buy the product or consume the service. I assume the consumer is only the who have stable basic income source consumer target. This stable basic income target consumers who will evaluate or feel they will earn more benefits than costs to every product in their consumption process, after they will make final decision to choose to buy the product to use or consume the service. Otherwise, if they feel they won't earn more benefits after they buy the product or consume the service in the consumption process. Then, they won't choose to buy the product to use or consume the service. In behavioral economic view point, it indicates their consumption behaviors are depend on comparing the product or the service whether it can satisfy their desire benefits and their desire benefits to the product or service must be more than their consumption cost.

There are four points to apply consumer psychological time method to predict each stable basic income individual income spending. They include: motivation, conspicuous consumption, social preferences and crowding theory.

Each stable basic income consumer individual spending amount will be different and it is represent that every high stable basic income consumer must decide to consume any high cost services or buy high cost products to use. Although some economic teachers assume general high income people will accept to spend more expenditures for enjoyment or buy high cost of products to satisfy basic high level necessary expenditures. But, applying behavioral economic analysis, it is not absolute true, some low income people also accept to spend more to buy high cost of products or increasing spending expenditures for enjoyment for their basic necessary expenditures.

The field of consumer psychological time seems to behavioral economic can be fined as a combination of economics and consumer psychological time that tries to capture human behavior in a more realistic. Understanding each consumer individual consumption behavior, we need to know how who does each decision to influence each consumption choice. Consequently, analysis reaches the conclusion. Every high or low level stable basic income consumer individual behavioral consumption that the microeconomic consequences of a stable basic income of individual consumer target consumption group could be efficiency enhancing, but at the same time incentives about positional concerns could lead to wasteful and inefficient spending to the stable low basic income consumer target group.

How to apply consumer psychological time method to contribute to the stable basic income target consumer group's consumption prediction?

What is basic income mean? A basic income is an income paid by a political community to all its members on an individual basis, without means test or work requirement. How to apply behavioral economic method to contribute to the basic income consumption prediction?

I assume high income tax is charged to one high income tax payee , it will influence the high income tax payee individual consumption desires to be fallen, also extrinsic incentives will effort and intrinsic motivation and how the labor market change these variables under and big changes predicting, how income security changes social consumption preferences, e.g. how a big change affects the overall level of status -seeking behavior and this effect with income inequality to influence consumer individual consumption attitude or habit.

How can consumer psychological time methods predict consumer's consumption decision, in special the stable basic income consumer target group? In any consumption decisions are involving risk and uncertainty, the standard economic model usually assumes that decisions are based on final condition, regardless of the changes are caused by the results of a consumer's decision.

An alterative mode of how consumers make decision and judgement under risk and uncertainty. This situation is often occurred in consumption market.

In consumer psychological time view point, it explains how consumer's consumption, however, which excludes the stable basic income earn factor can influence the stable basic income earn target consumer group decides to make final consumption decision to compare to the non-stable basic income earn target consumer group. The reasons include as below:

(1) Consumers evaluate decisions over gains and losses with respect to some natural reference point, when they feel need to consume, which is assumed to be judgement about a sequence of outcomes are based on changes in wealth, rather than whether how much absolute basic income earn to influence whose consumption desires.

(2) Thus, consumer psychological time or behavioral economic theory assumes the consumer is the low level of income group in society, but when who feels that he is still gains more than losses when who decides to buy the expensive product or consumes the expensive service. Then, the low level of income consumer who will accept to buy the expensive product or

consume the service easily. Due to whose gains feeling is more than losses feeling, when who buys the product or consumes the service.

(3) Behavioral economic or consumer psychological time theory also assume the taxpayer will pay high income tax in this year. The, even the high income taxpayer can earn high basic income, but due to whom needs to pay high income tax in this year. Then, he/she will reduce much spending, even he/she reduces spending on cheap products or cheap service consumption for enjoyment. This is the taxpayer's economic decision to influence whose consumption behavior, due to the high income tax expenditure factor influences whose consumption behavior to change to be reduced spending expenditures in this year.

How to apply organizational psychological time method to predict labor market changing behavior?

Instead of applying behavioral economic method to predict every consumer individual consumption effort. Behavioral economic method can be also be applied to predict every country's labor market changing behavior. Particularly, how salary clerical workers or low wage labor workers should move from one type of job to another based on these factors. They include as below:
Their intrinsic motivation and how their levels of effort would change after this movement, investigates the effects of income security on social preferences in labor market changing behavior, and how cooperation in social contribution is affected when income security is guaranteed, how to predict the role of positional externalities on conspicuous consumption and how would change the incentive to influence consumption. So, it seems that general labor market job changing behaviors will not influenced by external economic environment better or worse changing factor, or salary changing factor etc. different environmental condition changing factors influence to employees' job changing. Generally, employee's job changing behavior is more influenced to persuade who changes job by himself/herself intrinsic motivation negative emotion influence mainly.
How to apply motivation crowding theory to predict labor productivity? One of the main challenges of economic theory is to find what are the optimal incentives that increase productivity of labors. The standing point is usually extrinsic incentive be it is form of monetary compensations for high effort or fine for low effort.
It is a kind method of reward or punishment to increase or decrease number of productivity to every labor. But it can only raise short term number

of productivity in possible and it can not guarantee high quality of productivity. So if one employer wants a labor to do more of an activity or with a higher quality, consider paying the labor for working hard on punishing whom if for providing a low level effort.

This idea is that people do not like to work, and therefore they used some sort of compensation for doing a specific activity, and that the more they are paid the harder, they will work. So, payment better compensation is only beneficial to encourage labors to do one specific task or activity in short term. This method can not be suitable to rise long term beneficial productivity and high level quality of production or excellent performance in long term and it can only keep in short term raising productivity and high level quality of production or excellent performance benefits.

Consider paying the labor for working hard on punishing whom if for providing a low level effort. This idea is that people do not like to work, and therefore they used some sort of compensation for doing a specific activity, and that the more they are paid the harder they will work. So, payment better compensation is only beneficial to encourage labors to do one specific task or activity in short term. This method can not be suitable to raise long them beneficial productivity and high quality of products.

However, economists would argue that, is a labor has high intrinsic motivative to perform a task, who will provide a high level of effort without compensation by himself/herself but an even higher level of effort of whom is compensated. If a labor does not have any intrinsic motivation to perform a task or an activity, who will provide no effort or a low effort of whom. There is no compensation, but who will increase this level of effort of an extrinsic incentive is implemented.

Hence, in behavioral economic view point, the labor individual high level effort is a main psychological factor to influence whose productivity to be raised or the qualities of products to be raised, when the products are manufactured by the high level effort labor. It means that high compensation is not the good method to encourage labor productivity or raise quality. Otherwise, how to influence the one low level of effort of labor to change to be one high level of effort labor. It is the best psychological method to influence the labor to raise productivity and quality and service performance to any products or services in manufacturing process or service process for any organizations in long term beneficial possible.

How can apply consumer psychological time method raises basic stable income consumer consumption desire?

Economists aim to develop models of human behavior and interactions in consumption markets. But consumers behave in complex ways, such as how to predict consumers to make rational decisions in consumption processes. Moreover, self-consumption control and motivation can vary significantly across different individual consumer.

In order to build useful consumption prediction models, economists make simplifying assumptions, aims to predict how to raise stable basic income consumer target group consumption more success. However, behavioral economy method is one kind of accurate consumption prediction method. It can be applied to predict economic decision-making to every consumer consumption choice more accurate raising whose consumption desire?

I shall indicate how to apply different behavioral economy methods to raise stable basic stable income target consumer group consumption desire in these different consumption situation ( consumption environment) aspects as below:

1. Stable basic stable income consumer group consumption great or small amount desire

The consumption of products and services is a fundamental part of consumer's welfare. Basically, every one who has stable basic stable income, who will like to consume any products and services. Even, consumption great or small amount desire won't be depended on whether the person whose income is more or less. It means low income level of people will still like to consume great amount to buy expensive products or consume expensive services, because consumption is human's part of life and basic needs.

This stable basic income people will like to consume, because they have stable income source when they do not worry about unemployment occurrence to cause them have no enough money to support their life. Otherwise, non-stable basic stable income people won't like to consume because they feel they have no stable basic income source to support their life and they will worry about unemployment occurrence any time. Hence, stable basic income people will have more consumption desire to compare non-stable basic stable income people in any countries usually. Behavioral economic method indicates they feel their economic benefits will be loss if they planned to buy any products or consume any services easily. So, they prefer to save money in bank more than consumption.

1. Demand systems and micro-economic factor influence basic income people consumption attitude

Why stable basic income people will like to consume? Because who have more demand, a demand system shows the level of consumer demand for different products and services: e.g. one basic stable income person may refer to the demand for clothes, another the demand for food etc.

How the demand for that particular product varies with the prices and demographic factor will influence who to accept consumption. Such as stable basic income people who will not consider to decide to buy the cloth to wear or the food to eat if who feel the cloth or food price is even more expensive to compare other kind of cloth or food.

Otherwise, non-stable basic income people who will consider to decide to buy the cloth to wear or the food to eat if they feel that they still have enough cloths to wear or enough food to eat at homes , even these food or cloth price are less expensive to compare others. Because they feel they lack stable income effort to support them to consume. Hence, basic stable income factor can influence the consumer's consumption decision.

2. Life-cycle advertisement method can influence consumer individual consumption behaviors to be increased

Consumer behavior makes strong assumptions about the informational and computational bases of consumer behavior. Generally, consumer behavior is reasonably characterized as the maximization of expected lifetime utility subject to budget constraint and conditional on the available information.

Generally, consumers prefer to buy any discounted products or it is reasonable that consumers accept to buy many attractions to persuade them to buy any kinds of bargain discount products. Hence, low bargain discount product is one good behavioral economic principle to encourage or persuade or attract any consumers to increase consumption.

What is behavioral life-cycle model? This model explains consumer behavior can be persuaded to buy any discounted products by advertisement, e.g. television, radio, newspapers, magazine etc. promotion channels. Because frequent advertisement promotion method can let any consumers often remember the product's brand, discounted price, style, color and image from advertisement content.

So, advertisement can be one part of consumer behavioral life-cycle. For example, when the television audiences often watch TV. Hence, when the brand of product advertisement often makes fun image and discounted message to let TV audiences to remember this brand of product, when they are watching TV. Then, it has possible to persuade any potential consumers to choose to buy this brand of any products or consume this brand of any services, due to its advertisement of discounted sale message is very attractive to every one to let this advertisement audience's attention to remember this brand of products or services are selling or serving in market at this moment. So, it is advertisement image behavior influences audiences to buy the brand's any products attractively and persuasively.

3. Raising electricity consumption from electricity user individual habit

For electricity use market case example, how to analyze people's behavior in consuming electricity using a behavioral economic framework ? Electricity consumption is modeled by the means of consumer's individual useful habit, electricity price, consumer satisfaction level, willingness to invest in new technologies, social interactions, and marketing strategies by the power utility. Because electricity is necessary to every home or electric vehicle users needs or businessmen office etc. different needs every day.

Power companies supply electricity to a region's homes and industries. However, electricity needs modernization of power system companies expect to increase price. Due to competitive factor, such as other fuel resource choices, outdated kind of energy electricity supply, and renewable fuel energy source competition.

Hence, applying behavioral economic concept, I assume electricity consumers will compare to electricity and other kinds of energy choices to weigh up the costs and benefits of all alternatives, aiming to maximize their benefits, before making a decision to choose to use electricity for their house electricity demand or electric vehicle or shop or factory manufacturing etc. function of different aspects of electricity users.

For example, electricity business clients, they aim to reduce cost, such as energy expenditure, when they use any energy to manufacture their products in factories. If they feel electricity is expensive price to compare other kinds of energy power supply. When, they feel that they can not earn much beneficial advantages to use electricity to produce their products. Otherwise, if they feel other any kinds of energy supply can replace electricity to give more benefits to compare electricity energy. Then, many business electricity users will change to use other kinds of energies to consume to replace electricity power.

However, electricity can have competitive ability in electric vehicles market, if many drivers feel environment protection is more important to compare vehicles will be popular to be driven, due to many drivers don't want air pollution. They will like gas vehicles. Hence, the main attribute from the consumer side is one their habit electricity consumption behaviors, satisfaction level, energy efficient interaction with the power utility.

Consequently how to predict electricity consumer's demand. The important factor is how to let electricity users to feel power companies are changing a reasonable level to compare other similar energy supply products. When electricity users feel electricity which can bring more benefits to compare other kinds of energy products. Then, in energy supply market, if the demanding number of electricity consumers can increase more than other kinds of energy demanding number. Then, it is right time to raise electricity price to charge electricity consumers. Hence, how to persuade electricity consumers to feel that they can have more benefits to compare other kinds of energy products. It is the main successful factor to electricity power supply companies.

Consumer confidence is as a predictor of consumption spending when consumer feels have enough time to consume

Behavioral economists believe it has link between confidence and economic decisions to cause consumers to choose spending, if the consumer has confidence to believe the product is worth to use, then who will accept to buy the product to use.

Concentrated on the conceptualization of confidence and its role in mode in theories of consumption. It also concerns on whether the confidence indicators contain any information beyond economic fundamentals. The concern is whether confidence can be explained by current and past value of variables, such as income, unemployment, inflation or consumption or in other way.

Whether confidence measures have any statistical significance in predicting economic outcomes once information from the above variables is used. Economic variable factor will also influence consumer confidence to decide consumption spending, e.g. real consumption expenditures ( income, wealth or interest rate).

Finally, it will identify under which circumstances confidence indicates can be a good predictor of household consumption. Hence, survey is one good measurement method to predict whether how much every household has confidence to spend to consume the brand of products to use. Why is survey a good confidence consumption measurement prediction to every household in every country?

The reasons include survey can gather every household consumption habit history data to evaluate whether every survey person has how much confidence to consume the brand of products. Which in most cases correspond to periods where there are large changes in household survey indicators, liking during financial crises or geopolitical tensions to measure or predict whether the country's future good or bad economic condition factor will influence every household consumption desire in the year.

This modelling approach assumes that there is a certain ( unknown) in confidence index changes beyond which confidence starts impacting consumption behaviors. So, sample household surveys can show the contribution of confidence in explaining consumption expenditures increases when household survey indicators feature large changes. So that confidence indicators can have some increasing predictive power during the survey investigation period in the year.

Other view point, surveys have been concerned on whether the confidence indicators contain any information beyond economic fundaments. The concern is whether confidence can be explained by current and past values of variables, such as income, unemployment, inflation or consumption or the other way. Whether confidence measures have any statistical significance in predicting economic outcomes once information from different external variable factors to influence the survey household group.

What is confidence in consumption survey ?

Confidence in consumption. For example, to measure whether how much degree of strong inflation in the economy, such as recessions and recoveries will influence the country's household confident consumption in the year.

The surveys consumers' questions usually concern on major expenditures and changes in the respondent's financial situation, focus on job availability and current business conditions etc. questions. It is then possible that about consumer confidence depending on the relative performance of the variables that may be more relevant balances, with respect to the factors that determine unemployment and other labor market related issues. It aims to investigate whether those any one of variable factors will influence consumers general loss confident consumption desire in this year.

What is a confidence indicator ?

A confidence indicator is considered as an explanatory variable for consumption together with standard variables used on predicting consumption expenditure. However, the natural real personal consumption expenditure is unexpected and unpredicted easily.

In conclusion, consumption expenditure depends the consumer individual confidence. If the consumer has much confidence to feel this year economic change will be better and he/she is easily to find job, then he/she will accept consumption easily in this year. It seems financial wealth and unemployment etc. economic factors will influence every household consumption desire. So, survey is one kind of good psychological consumption prediction method to predict consumption spending for any country in the year. I recommend manufacturers may choose to apply survey method to attempt to enquire sample survey people to gather data to predict whether what degree of consumption desire to them and find solution methods to solve low degree of consumption desire challenge.

Reference

Camerer, C.F. Babrocks, Loewenstein, G., & Thaler, R. (1997). Labor supply of New York city candrivers: One day of a time. The Quacterly Jounrnal of economics, 112 (2), 407-441. doi: 10.1162/003355399555244.

How do you view the outlook for consumer confidence in your key markets next year? Source from : http://www.Just-food.com Confidence survey, Nov.2015


Jim. P. & Brendan. M. ( 2013) . What I learned losing a million dollars, p.160. Colimbia University, Columbia business school press, New York, US.

Kamenica, E. (2012). Behavioral economics and psychology of incentives. Annual review of economics, 4 (1), 427-452. doi: 10.1146/ annurev- economics-080511-110909.

Maselli, 2012 Technology driven job polarization in EU , 2000-2010. % change in labor supply skilled/upgrade (ISCED) and labor demand for skills/tasks (ISOD).

# CHAPTER SIX

# Consumer behavioral factors influence theory

To research consumer behavior, it has different theory to explain why and how the consumer is influenced to make the choice by different factors. For example, utility theory,it explains that consumers make choices based on the expected outcomes of their decisions. They are viewed as rational decision makers and they only consider self interest.

Utility theory views consumer is as a " rational economic man". However, the factors influence consumer behaviors may include these activities, such as need recognition, information search, evaluation of alternatives, the building of purchase intention , the act of purchasing choice, consumption and finally disposal. Hence, it seems that all the consumer's activities in whose purchase processes. They will influence their choice. For example, when the property purchase consumer , he plans to research different kinds of properties information concern price, location, housing areas, room numbers, building facilities and environment facilities. He will find some sample target properties information to make comparison in order to decide to buy which of property is the most suitable to satisfy his living need.

However, it is not only one activity for the property purchase buyer in his decision making process. It also include evaluation of alternatives activity when he ensures the accurate property information number in order to evaluate whether which one of all these property choices is the most suitable one. Hence, it explains that property information research and evaluation of alternatives both activities are needed to spend much time for this property buyer. If he does not plan to find one property to live in short time, it is possible that he can spend one month, even more than one month or more than three months time to do the only property information gathering activity.

Hence, it seems that time factor is not the main factor to influence the property buyer to do property purchase decision immediately. Otherwise, if the property buyer plans to find one new property to live within one month. Then, time factor is possible one important factor to influence this property purchase choice decision. For example, if he felt that he needs more time to spend to gather information concerns the large house area size and the properties have more than three bathrooms and/or bedrooms properties information. Then, he will be possible not to find any this kinds of all property information. So, it means that all these properties won't be his choice. It is because long time property information gathering activity factor influence.

I assume that the property buyer is a economic man and he does not spend much time to do the property information gathering activity. So, this kind of property needs him to spend long time to gather properties information in order to make this kind of properties comparison. Moreover, because he expects to live one new property within one month. So, he only chooses the properties, they have less than three bedrooms and/or bathrooms to gather sample properties information in order to make property purchase decision within one month. Hence, the time variable factor can only influence the property purchaser when he/she needs to make decision to buy one new property to live in the short time. If some kinds of properties choices number has a lot and the property buyer feels to let that he/she must need to spend long time to find the suitable properties number to make evaluation alternatives comparison behavior.

Then, the time variable limiting pressure factor will be possible the main factor to influence the property buyer's choice in order to make the most suitable kind of property purchase decision. Hence, it is one case example of how time limiting pressure factor can influence consumer purchase choice decision, such as property purchases market case. The reason explains why the property buyer needs to spend time to do property information gathering. I assume that general property buyer behave rationally in the economic sense. They won't only believe property agent individual property photos advertisement , it concerns where the property location is and facility etc. information on property photos in order to evaluate whether the property price is reasonable to pay. Generally, property buyers need to attempt to gather property information and visit the different actual property locations to make choice. So, general property consumers would have to be aware of all the available different kinds of properties consumption options from themselves properties information gathering and the properties agents' verbal properties introduction both be capable of correctly rating each property alternative and the available to select the optimum course of the final property purchase action.

Hence, in the property purchase and sold market, limiting time pressure factor will be important influential factor to decide whether the kinds of properties will be option to some property buyers when they feel need to find one suitable property to buy in short time. Otherwise, in some food consumption market , time limiting pressure factor will not be the main factor to influence consumer option. Such utility theory indicates consumers are as one rational economic man, whom do not expect to spend much time to do any options evaluation decision making.

However, in coffee market, buying a coffee comes almost automatically and does not need much information search. Hence, time limiting pressure factor won't one main factor to influence coffee consumer to choose to buy the kind of coffee to drink. However, there are other factors to influence coffee consumers' kind of coffee drinking option from cultural, social, personal or psychological factors. So, coffee taste producer can follow these factors to estimate how coffee consumers might behave in the future when making any kinds of coffee making purchasing decisions.

Firstly, social factor can affect coffee consumer behavior significantly. Every coffee consumer has someone around influencing his/her coffee buying decisions. The important social factors include reference groups, family, role and status , e.g. when the coffee buyer has high income job and his friends have good educational level and high income. Then, he will compare his reference group, such as his friends' coffee buying behavior choosing which kinds of coffee taste to drink in habits or lifestyles. If he chooses the kind of coffee taste to drink, its price is cheaper to compare his friends' drinking coffee tastes. Then, he may be influenced to follow his friends to drink the same kinds of coffee taste in order to keep their same social status and role between him and his friends.

Secondly, the coffee consumers will be influenced how to choose which kinds tastes of coffee to drink by personal factors, such as his age, life cycle state, occupation, economic situation , lifestyle and personality and self-concept. Age related factors are such as taste in food, e.g. the kinds of coffee taste. Although, coffee price is cheap, but if the coffee consumer's income is more and he/she can often spend to buy different kinds of taste coffees to drink. Then, his/her income level will have much purchasing power to influence his/her purchasing behavior. Hence the coffee consumer's frequency of consumption of different kinds of coffee taste drinking choice behavior will represent whether his/her income level is high or low in possible. For example, the consumer needs to go to automatic coffee shop to buy at least three cups or more different kinds of high class good taste coffee brands to drink per week. Although, these high class coffee brands' prices are higher than the low class of coffee brands. But the coffee consumer still only buys any one of these kinds of high class brands' coffee taste to drink. Hence, it seems that this coffee consumers ought have high income to let him to buy at least three cups of high class brand of coffee taste to drink from automatic coffee ship per week.

So, income factor can influence the coffee consumer to choose either coffer purchase from supermarket or coffee drinking at automatic coffee shop. If the coffee consumer only chooses to buy coffee from supermarket, due to the bottles of different kinds of brand coffee can provide more different tastes of coffees choices from shelves to let him to buy to drink at home. So, it seems that the coffee consumer's income level is low in general. Otherwise, if the coffee consumer only chooses to go to automatic coffee shop to buy the high class brands of coffee tastes to drink at least three times or more per week. It may mean that the coffee consumer has high income level to support him/her to often go to automatic coffee shop to buy different kinds of high class coffee tastes to drink frequently every week. Some high or low income level factor can influence every coffee consumer individual drinking coffee behavioral options.

Moreover, when the coffee consumer is younger coffee consumer will be possible to buy much coffee to drink. Because younger age people can accept to drink coffee habitually more than older age people. Also, it is possible that younger people feel often drinking coffee behavior will help them to bring more health feeling and /or raising nervous to learn , due to they need often to go to schools to study. Otherwise, older age people feel often drinking coffee behaviors won't help them to bring more health and they do not need to raise nervous to learn.

Finally, even, cultural difference factor will influence coffee consumers number for any countries. For example, western countries' people like to drink any kinds of coffee tastes traditionally. Asia countries' people like to drink any different kinds of teas tastes traditionally. So, different kinds of teas tastes will be Asia people's traditional drinking substitute to replace different kinds of coffee tastes more easily. Hence, culture difference will be one factor to influence Asia coffee buyers number. So, it seems that time limiting pressure factor won't influence coffee consumers' coffee taste choices to different kinds of high class or low class brands, visiting coffee shops or visiting supermarkets choices, frequent or not frequent coffee drinking behaviors.

How and why time limiting pressure
influences consumer choice

Can consumer buying decisions be influenced by time limiting pressure. For these three situations, they will influence consumer hoe makes different buying decision, e.g. in the little time available, but the consumer needs to do more effort needed to choose to buy which kind of product among variety kinds of product choice or in a moderate amount of time available, or a considerable amount of time available. In this first situation, the consumer can not real attempt to find any weaknesses or unique characteristics of the products, because it has no enough time to allow whom to choose. So, his/her product evaluation won't be the most accurate to satisfy his/her needs because little time can only allow him/her to find some weaknesses of the products. Otherwise, in the final situation, because the consumer has a considerable amount of time to allow him/her to attempt to find the weaknesses and/or strengths characteristics of the products choice. So, he/she ought do the more reasonable or accurate evaluation of these products to choose the most effective economic beneficial product to buy. Thus, it seems that time limiting pressure factor can influence the consumer to make more rational or more reasonable economic beneficial consumption decision making to buy the product or consume the service.

Thus, a consumer buying decision will require these situations to do buying decisions, they may include either little time and conscious effort or a moderate amount of time and effort or a considerable amount time and effort. The products may include cheap products/services , e.g. fruit, DVD, university courses, computers, facial services, surgeries, sport shoes, reference books, soft drinks, magazines as well as expensive products/ services, e.g. cars, houses, luxury goods, e.g. jeweler, female hand bags, holiday travelling entertainment. So, any expensive or cheap products or services, the consumer will need to spend either little or moderate or considerable amount time to do gathering information about the different kinds of products or services in order to find which brand of product or service can bring more economic benefit when he/she chooses to use the product or consume the service. He/she will compare his/her preference sample brands limiting number of products or services choices to decide to buy the brand of product or consume the brand service easily. However in the consumer's consuming decision making process, he/she will need to spend either little or moderate or a considerable amount of time to do the evaluation and choice consumption behavior. It means that time limiting pressure factor will influence the consumer how to make consumption choice consequently.

What are the impacts of reduced branding on consumer choice and time limiting pressure to influence consumer behavior? When one consumer needs to choose products to buy one in a time limiting pressure consumption environment, when branding on packaging is reduced, e.g. the brand of product has 10 different style of packages to let consumer choice, but it reduces to only 5 different style of packages to let consumer choice. How does it influence the consumer decision making when the consumer has little time to allow to choose these 5 different style of packages ? For example, when the consumer expects to spend only 10 minutes to choose any one style of package to buy this brand product. Currently, this brand of product has reduced different style of packages number from 10 to 5. Do you feel that the consumer will feel easy to do decision making to choose to buy the most attractive style of package product from this brand's 5 different style of packages choices? Is 10 minutes consumption choice time enough to let the consumer to make final purchase decision from these brand's 5 different style of packages choice? Will the time limiting pressure be reduced , due to this brand's 10 style packages are reduced to 5 style packages to let the consumer to choose within the 10 minutes expected limiting consumption choice time.

It is one interesting psychological consumption behavior to research whether the brand's reducing different style of packages number factor will influence the consumer to do the decision making in the short time in the time limiting pressure environment. For toothpaste, shapmoo products example, if the brand of these products' style packages choice is reduced to 5 style packages from 10 style packages choice. When one consumer finds the brand of toothpaste or shampoo has only 5 style packages on the shelves in supermarket. If the consumer has moderate or considerate amount time to let him/her to choose these both kinds product any one style of packages to buy. The 5 style packages to these both of products will be impossible to satisfy the consumer's choice need because he/she has much time to stay in supermarket to choose. Otherwise, if the consumer has little time to allow to stay in the supermarket , e.g. only 10 minutes. Then, he/she expects to spend only 10 minutes consumption choice time to do buying decision making within 10 minutes. These both kinds of the brand's products, its style of packages choice number is reduced to 5, it is possible to satisfy the consumer's choice need to buy this brand of product either toothpaste or shampoo and both of thee brand of products to be chose to buy in the supermarket. So , the reducing style of package number to let consumer choice will be seem to let the consumer to do buying decision making in the limiting time pressure consumption environment.

In fact , package is such a visual to influence consumer decision making in the short time or personal limiting time choice process. If the product has more attractive package design, the it can bring more attention effort to influence the consumer to choose to buy the product in the short time information transfers to influence the consumer decision making to choose to buy more easily , when he/she is active in communication process. So, package, communicating with consumer in the selling place , has become an essential factor to influence the choice of consumer.

Scientific researches have proved that package decisions can attract consumer attention, transfer the desirable information about the product, position , the product in consumer conscious, differentiate and identify of among similar kinds of products. In that way elements of package influence consumer decision making process and can determine the choice of consumer and the package itself can become more competitive advantage.

However it is not absolute that the brand of product has more package choices, it must have more customers to choose to buy its product. For example, there are two brands of shampoo in the supermarket shelf. One brand shampoo has 5 different style of packages and 5 different fruit productive elements to cause similar fresh fruit smells to attract consumers to buy. Another brand shampoo has 3 different style of packages and 3 different fresh fruit smells to attract consumers to buy in the same shelf location also. When one supermarket customer has little time to expect to stay in the supermarket, e.g. he expects only to stay the supermarket maximum to 15 minutes. he expects to buy one bottle shampoo and meats and fruits and vegetable within 15 minutes. Hence, he expects only to spend about 5 minutes to choose one brand of shampoo product as well as he demands to spend maximum 10 minutes to buy other foods within

15 minutes. When he stays in the sham shelf location, he finds only two brands of shampoo products are displayed on the same shelf location. One brand of shampoo has 5 different style packages to let him to choose, but he feels that these 5 different style packages are not very attractive. Otherwise, the another brand of shampoo has only 3 different style packages to let him to choose, but he feels that the 3 different style packages are very attractive. Due to he feels time causes pressure to choose these two brands of shampoo immediately. So, he does not want to spend more time more than 5 minutes to choose on brand of shampoo to buy. He will be influenced by the brand of different styles of packages more attraction to influence his buying decision making obviously. So, whether the shampoo brand's package is attractive or not, it will influence the consumer's buying decision making to choose either to buy the brand's shampoo product in preference.

So, the more packages choice to the brand's product which may not mean that it has high opportunity to influence consumers' attention. Otherwise, the attractive package element if more important to compare right number of packages choices. Consumer package can influence these elements, e.g. colour, size, imageries, graphics, materials, smell, brand name, producer/country, information, special offers. Of the brand of products can have much attractive elements. Then, it can attract consumers to choose to buy the brand's attractive package products in short time decision making process, such as perception of needs, search for information , evaluation of alternatives, decision making, behavior after purchase. Such as supermarket case, I assume that any supermarket consumers do not expect to spend much time to choose which brand of product is the most suitable or earning more economic benefit to buy when they need to stay the shelf to need spend much time to select which brand of product to buy in the supermarket. Because in general, supermarket consumers ought plan to buy more than one kind of product or food, even more usually. So, limiting time pressure factor will influence their decision making. Similarly, as my explanation indicates why although, the product had attractive package elements and its has many packages number choices, but it does not mean that it can win the similar product which has not more attractive packages, even it has more packages choices number to let supermarket consumers to choose. So, an attractive package element factor will have more influential and potential to cause supermarket consumers to choose to buy it in the supermarket limiting time pressure consumption environment.

How the time consumption pressure
factor influences irrational consumption
decision making

When one consumer has a large number of options, he/she will feel time pressure to cause whose accurate and reasonable evaluation. Then, the personal time limiting pressure factor will bring these questions: How does the time limiting pressure influence the consumer evaluation? Will the consumer personal limiting time pressure bring advantages and / or disadvantages in whom consumption decision making? How to help the consumer to solve short time decision problem when he/she encounters extreme time pressure and choice overload?

I shall assume every consumer is general one economic man. He/she feels time is important, he /she does not want to spend much time to choose one brand of product to buy among a number of brands of products choices. I also assume that any consumers decision making satisfaction, which is based on search until they found a sufficiently good item, or run not of time. So, it seems that which the consumer needs to buy one kind of product, but the product has a lot number of different brands to let the consumer to choose. The consumer ought need to spend much time to make choice decision making. However, consumer is one economic man, he/she ought not to search all different brands to decide whether which brand of product can bring the much economic value or utility value to choose to buy. So, in general, consumers will only choose sample brands of products to decide to buy the satisfied brand of product. For example, when the consumer needs to buy one television. The television has 20 brands of similar televisions to let he to choose. He will not spend much time to search these similar 20 televisions information. He will only gather sample 10 to 15 or less different brands of televisions to compare what their strengths and weaknesses, unique characteristics. Then, he will make decision to choose to buy the best television from these sample televisions. Hence, in general, consumers will feel time pressure when they feel need to spend much time to choose a lot different brands of similar products. Because they feel time is not enough to let they can do other important matters when they need to spend much time to do search information behavior when they need to buy any products usually. Hence, it is general consumers psychology that they will feel real choice under time pressure and choice overload, when they have too much a lot of similar brands of products to let them have opportunity to choose to make decision making to buy only one brand of product.

However, when a brand of product is familiar and given its simplicity and familiarity to general consumers' acknowledgement. It will have perference advantage to attract or influence consumers' attention or consideration. So, when the market has similar different brands of products are available to let consumers to choose. The largest choice set is not large enough to create overload to influence the brand's sale when consumers need to spend much time to choose these different brands similar products to buy. Because when the brand's any products are familiar and given its simplicity and familiarity to general consumers' knowledge. Then, it can build utility confidence to influence general consumers , it will be preference sample brand of product to do buying making option. Hence, the brand's familiarity factor will influence general consumers' preference buying decision making option. So, any product manufacturers need to concern how to build its brand familiarity to let many consumers to acknowledge in order to raise its competitive effort. Raising brand's familiarity may be a good method to solve consumer individual choice under time pressure overload , because when the brand of product is preference sample brand to any consumers. It's sale opportunity will also be raised. So, it brings the question: How can the brand of products can cause general consumers' preference choice. For food example, food brands were more likely to choose the implicitly preferred brand over the explicitly preferred one when choices were made under time pressure.

Imagining one customer enters a supermarket 10 minutes before closing time. He failed to write up a shopping list. So, when the staff is preparing to close store at the night, the consumer hurry not to for set too many of the ingredients for dinner . What brands of products , he opts for, as he can choose from a variety of similar foods, but time is short and the staff is looking at the consumer impatient? It is possible that the consumer will probably quickly decide in favor of the foods he likes best, pay, and leave the evening.

Hence, supermarket consumer's first time feeling to the brand of food will influence whom choice. One target category and one attribute category share same response key: Pleasant vs unpleasant feeing, if the supermarket consumer has pleasant feeling when he sees the food photos and touch the package of the brand of food to feel pleasant in the short supermarket closing time. Then, his pleasant feeling will be chooses to buy the brand of food to eat. Thus, the consumer individual pleasant or unpleasant feeling factor will influence whom consumption choice, such as this supermarket closing time pressure consumption.

In fact, many factors may influence whether consumer behavior is under more or less control. Hunger may influence control in the domain of eating behavior . So, such as the supermarket will close soon,it has store closing time pressure to influence the consumer needs hurry to make choice decision to buy food. If the consumer feels more hungry, he will not spend much time to find the right food to buy. He will be influenced by the different brand's food packages whether which brand of food package can bring a more pleasant to let him to feel, when he touch and sees the brand of food package. He won't spend time to search whether the different kinds of brands of foods have how much different health elements because the supermarket will close store soon. So, he only depends his individual pleasant feeling to make final food purchase decision. If he feels all of the kinds of brands foods are unpleasant food packages when he sees and touch them first time as well as he does not feel much hungry. Then, it is possible that he won't choose to any one food to eat. He will choose to go to restaurant to get dinner to replace buying food to cook to eat dinner at home at the night.

The another case is that time pressure concerns how on choice of information source impacts purchase decisions. When the consumer who buys one product , he needs to use the same number of information sources to search the product's information regardless of time pressure. Because he has more available time, he devotes more time , but only to selected the right sources to search information about the product. He will mostly use marketing dominant sources, e.g. magazine. he feels magazine can give more accurate information concerns to the product's good or bad quality real more reasonable and fair evaluation to let the consumer to acknowledge. so, when the consumer has much time to choose to buy which brand of product is the most best choice. He will buy magazine to find information. He believes magazine has more fair evaluation to different brands of product. It won't mislead consumers to make wrong decision making. Hence, in general, when consumers have much time to find information source to search which brand of product is more value to buy. They will attempt to buy consumer magazine to acknowledge whether the different brands of product , which have unique characteristics, strengths or weaknesses in order to compare them to make more accurate evaluation to choose to buy which brand of the kind product. When they have no time pressure to influence their choice process time to be shortened or reduced.

Otherwise, these consumers will depend on newspapers, television, radio advertisments information sources when they feel time pressure controls their consumption choice decision making process time to be shortened or reduced. Hence, time pressure will be possible to influence consumer individual information source channel choice.

Chapter Four
Time pressure consumption decision
making process characteristics

How we can predict or know the consumer time pressure in whom decision making process? Will it bring advantages or disadvantages to influence the businessmen benefits? I shall indicate some different consumption situations or environments to explain what will be impacted to sale number is increased or decreased to businesses when the consumer feel time pressure to avoid whom behavioral consumption to the product or the service.

Firstly, I shall explain that what effects of product popularity and time pressure on online shopping behaviors are . Electronic ecommerce is popular to any countries, in special, US, UK, China large areas countries, because when one customer feels need to spend one hour even more time to catch any transportation tool to arrive the shop to buy the kind of product. Then, due to far distance reason, he/she will choose to apply internet to buy the kind of product . If the seller has website to let the consumers to choose online shopping. However, it seems that online shopping behavior can reduce the consumer individual time pressure, when he/she feels need to catch any kinds of transportation tool to arrive the shop to buy the product. Moreover, when the consumer can turn on home computer to enter its website to choose the styles of the kind of products, which one is the most suitable to choose. He/she can spend time to search the different styles kinds of product information to compare and evaluate which brand of product will b whose purchase choice easily at home.

Hence, in psychological view, he/she can feel that spending time to search information from internet behavior which is more valuable and it can bring more economic benefit to make final purchase decision more than the behavior of spending long time to catch any transportation tools to visit the shop. Moreover, it is possible to bring failure risk that he/she wastes time to catch any transportation tools to visit the shop if he/she can not find any one of suitable product(s) to choose to buy. Hence, it seems the online shopping can influence the consumer reduced time pressure and wastes time to do any shopping decision.

This is online shopping's attractive strengths to the consumers when they need to spend long time to catch any kinds of transportation tools to visit the shop or when the consumer feels hurry to do other important matters, he/she can not allow himself/herself to spend long time to do his/her visiting the shop behavior. Moreover, another online shopping's advantage is that product popularity can be perceived by examining the information pre sended on websites. For example, research on online reviews confirms the review quantity presented with products become positively influences to consumers' purchase intention and it can persuade the online visitor can make decision to buy the product when he/she has enter the seller's online website to find the most suitable product to choose to buy more easily. Hence, it seems that it is more easy to persuade the online visitor to make final purchase decision more than visiting the shop , when the online visitor can attempt to do the click mouse behavior to enter the seller's online shop, such as website. Then, he/she will be influenced to view the seller's different kinds of colorful and attractive product pictures from the seller's website.

Consequently, it has much opportunity to persuade the consumer to do the final purchase decision. if the seller's website is attractive to persuade him/her to visit its website to find any new products more than five times, even tem times or every weak several times , even day one time frequently visiting behavior from internet channel. Hence, due to internet is convenient tool to let consumers to find any product information from the seller's website at home or public library , computer, or mobile phone. Consumers must find any product information any time in any places easily. So, online shopping can reduce any consumers' time pressure to visit any shops to expect to achieve final consumption decision aim in possible.

Thus, it seems that online shopping method can influence consumers to feel time saving and time pressure reducing consumption both advantages more than visiting shops' shopping method when the consumer is living far away from the shop. When the consumer feels that he/she is experiencing situational time pressure, then, he/she will respond well to seek another time saving situational consumption environment. So , it explains when one consumer feels he/she has no much time to catch long time transportation tool to visit the shop on the day. When he/she has computer at home, he/she will attempt to type the shop name to research whether it has online shopping platform service from internet. Because he/she does not want to spend one hour, even more time to catch transportation tool to arrive the shop, when he/she can't walk to the shop in short time. Even, he/she may feel online shopping behavior won't influence his/her eating , sleeping, or recreational time to be reduced at home or any places , when he/she can behave the online shopping behavior at home or any where conveniently.

Consequently, promoting online shopping is as a time-saver is likely to be effective for these experiencing situational time pressure. Those with situational pressure would almost certainly welcome anything that would reduce their activity level and the demands on their time. In fact, there is really no adult learning method for store shopping because it is something everyone learns to do from early childhood. But for many adult consumers, they feel have interest to learn how to use internet and web to shopping. Some adult will feel interest and it is value to learn how to use internet channel to anticipate the complexity of shopping online. For example, Super Walmart cheap food store that carries many thousands of products and brands to let online shoppers won't feel confused when viewing its online merchant's home page with only a few menu items and links from its website. So, Super Walmart website can let online shoppers to feel difficult that they can save much time to enter any merchants' home page . They only need to view the Super Walmart's website ,then they can find any preference cheap grocercies to compare and evaluate which one(s) is (are) value to buy. So, Super Walmart's website can let global cheap grocery online shoppers feel it can help them to save time to find any merchant's products from internet conveniently. Consequently, online shopping will be one popular time saving consumption channel to reduce time pressure to some consumers nowadays.

Secondly, I shall explain that what determines purchase decisions for airline tickets when the traveller fees time stress. When a travelling planner has no enough time to prepare whose travelling journey, whether the time stress will influence he/she feels decision difficulties and frustration, when it will cause he/she needs to gather significant amounts of information to lead to make to choose which airline ticket is the most right choice? How and number of airline options and time pressure influence the airline ticket buyer's purchase decision?

However, there are both kinds of time pressures to influence the airline ticket buyer's airline choice decision, they focus on either real decision deadlines ( physical time), such as the journey beginning day is any day of this week or tomorrow or subjective feeling of pressure with time ( sense of urgency or psychological time), such as the traveller expects that he/she fears all airlines' all seats are full booked in this month. Moreover, he/she can plan to catch air plane to travel next month. So, he/she will attempt to gather any airlines' tickets prices, flight day and time and destination arrival and weather information in this month to avoid that it is too late to delay his/her next month travelling plan.

Hence, it seems that the effect of number of airlines choices and air tickets purchase deadlines ( physical time limit) will influence how the traveller or air ticket buyer's purchase decision using secondary data to search of airline ticket. for example, if the traveller felt time is no enough to let him/her to go to travel agent to enquire any airlines' air tickets prices and seats and date and time air plan departure available time to concern the traveller's destination choice. Then, he/she will be probable to choose to buy electronic-ticket (e-ticket) from internet. If he/she has computer to link internet to gather any airlines' flying date and time and seat available information at home easily. Hence, it seems that one time pressure traveller will be probable to choose e-ticket purchase at home in preference. If the airline can provide online e-ticket purchase option to the time pressure traveller. Due to the pressure time traveller feels closer to departure, the negative impact of number of airline options is not as strong when he/she can view the airline's website to find the flight date, time and seat available information to purchase e-ticket to pre book the date and time to departure the traveller's country and to arrive his/her travelling destination information from the airline's website channel at home or anywhere any time conveniently. Hence, travel agency can bring a positive relationship between airline number of options and pre-booking airline that immediate possibility. When the time pressure traveller hopes the airline can build the good interactive relationship between number of options and decision time limit ( number of days till planned travel effort on e-ticket purchase probabilities. So, if the airline website can let the traveller to predict when date and time is accurate available to arrive whom frequently destination choice country as well as the e-ticket's real price , it is not e-ticket predictive price and the real seats number available, it is not the estimated seats number available on the departure time and date to the travelling or arrival country destination. Then, all of these online information to the airline, which will raise the e-ticket pre-booking purchase chance to let the e-ticket buyer to make whose final e-ticket purchase choice decision to win its e-ticket competitors easily.

Consequently, a real time e-ticket information can attract any time pressure e-ticket buyers to choose to buy its e-ticket ( electronic airline ticket) more than visiting travel agent's paper airline ticket option when the travel feels hurry to buy airline ticket to travel in short time.


Reducing time pressure consumption
methods

How can sellers persuade consumers to choose to buy their products or consume their services in time pressure environment easily? It is a valuable research topic to concern how to know how consumer individual decision making to spend his/her available resources ( time, money and efforts, or consumption relate aspects) as well as how any why he/she chooses the preference brand to buy its any kind of products or consume its services, when he/she chooses to buy the brand of products or consume its services? Hence, marketers need to obtain an in depth knowledge of consumer buying behavior.

In any buying process, time factor will have about 10 % to 40 % to influence consumer decision. When the consumer feels hurry to consume, e.g. planning to go to travel, when he/she needs to choose to buy which airline's air ticket and what day and time is the right air ticket pre booking purchase decision right time choice; or enrolling which school to be chose course to study decision, e.g. how long time is needed to be choose which school is the most suitable to provide the most suitable courses studying choice change; purchase warm clothes to wear in winter, when is the suitable time to choose to buy the cheaper warm cloths to prepare to wear in winter, e.g. Jan to Mar., April to June, July to Aug. month; when is the most suitable time to buy another new house to live, when the property consumer( buyer) has lived present house for long time, e.g. three years or more. All of these issues will include time factor to influence the consumer feels when he/she ought choose to buy the kind of product or consume the kind of service. However, the other factors will also include to influence his/ her decision, e.g. family, friend relationship factor, advertising factor, social status factor, cultural difference factor, personal psychological need level or satisfactory level factor, young or old age factor, income level factor, economic environment factor, material enjoyable need factor etc. factors.

However, time pressure factor will be the consumer individual intrinsic ( internal) psychological feeling factor, and it is the consumer individual intrinsic feeling to judge whether when he/she ought spend some money to buy the kind of new product or the kind of consume service ( what time is the most reasonable or the most suitable time) to make purchase choice decision. However, when the consumer feels hurry to make purchase decision. So, he/she will not hope to spend more time to gather more information to compare and evaluate which one is the right brand of product to choose to buy or the right service to consume among different brands of products or services. Otherwise, if the consumer has more time or he/she can make the decision to buy any brand of product. Then, he/she ought spend more time to gather more information to compare and evaluate which one is the most suitable product choice to buy or which one is the right service choice to consume. So, time pressure factor will have some influence to any consumers to make decision about what time is the suitable time to buy the kind of product or consume the service. For example, heater product is usually when winter weather time, the heater products need number ought increase in winter weather time or season. But, it is possible that the heater products need number won't increase in winter season / weather possible, when one country , there are many householders or families , they have one heater number at least at home. Then, it is possible that these householders or families won't have consumption desires to buy one more heater product to use in winter at home, because they have had one heater to use at home in winter. So , when the country has have many customers number, they are using the kind of heater products at homes. Most people own at least one heater number factor will have possible to influence enough time available to cause they do not feel hurry to buy any heaters to use at homes, so, their do not feel time pressure to buy any heaters in short time. Because they do not plan to buy the kind of product to use at home in short time when they have one heater product at least to use at homes in present.

Hence, it brings this question: How to attract or persuade the customers, they are using the kind of product to let they feel time pressure to make decision to buy another new or same brand of product to replace to use? The product's better quality , long durable time useful, brand loyalty and past good purchase experience factors will influence him/her to feel time pressure to need to buy another new product in short time. So, when the consumer feel time pressure to make decision to purchase, he/she will choose when is the most right time to gather information, search, select, use and dispose of another new product to replace the old product in the short time.

Hence, the brand of product needs have good product motives, may be raised to the consumer's impluse, desires, considerations which make the buyer purchase the brand's new product to replace the present using product in order to achieve whose satisfactory needs to emotional product motives and rational product motives both. Moreover, persuading or encouraging the consumer feels he/she has real need to buy the kind of new product or replace the present old product (s), the brand of product marketer needs let the consumer feels these any one of nature of motive to raise his/her purchase decision desire in time pressure environment. The natures of motive may include: When the consumer feels desire for saving money, he/she will choose to buy it when the brand of product falls down, when he/she feels fear to be sickness, retirement, he/she will choose to buy insurance policy, when he/she feels pride, or high social status knowledge, he/she will buy premium product , e.g. gold, expensive watch, car , when he/she feels fashion need, he/she will move house to live from rural to urban, or rural people imitate urban to learn to do their fashion living behavior, when he/she feels possession need, he/she will feel need to buy antiques for its future unique worth satisfactory feeling in possible, when he/she feels health need, he/she will choose to buy health foods, join membership in health clubs, when he/she needs to enjoy comfortable feeling, he/she will feel need to buy micro-oven, washing machine to use at home, when he/she feels love and affection need, he/she will buy gift items to give to whose friends or families for presents in their birthday or lover day etc. special days to let they to feel happy. So, when the marketer can touch the consumer individual different nature of motives to satisfy his/her personal purchase feeling need and it can know how to influence them to feel that they have these any one of purchase motive needs in short time. Then, they will be persuaded to raise time pressure to make purchase decision to buy any kind of products in short time.

However, instead of attractive good product quality method can attempt consumers to make time pressure consumption behavior. The another method is brand loyalty building method, which can be attempted to encourage or persuade consumers to feel consumption desire need to make decision to buy the brand of any products in time pressure consumption environment. For example, when the consumers feel the brand is loyalty and it can build good image to his/her feeling , and this time pressure factor can influence this brand of any products which has high discount price to attract the consumer individual attention , e.g. familiar brand high class cars, the good confident house agent's high class houses, and the expensive and infrequently buying items, come under this category. When their prices are fallen down to sell cheaper , e.g. twenty per cent discount or more than twenty percent discount sale price than the other similar competitive brands' any products' normal prices. Then, it is possible to let these expensive items' consumers have high involvement and high feeling need in time pressure consumption environment. Because they assume that this discount sale price will be short time sale price, e.g. after three months or next month etc. short time discount sale price in short time period. Then, these expensive items' prices will be raised to the normal sale price, even higher price. so, they have time pressure feeling to feel that it is right time to make consumption decision in order to avoid to lose these low price purchase benefit in this non-predictive cheap discount price purchase items. so, if the expensive item marketer can build long time good brand loyalty relationship to consumers. Then, it will have much influential effort to persuade consumers feel consumption desires need by its any extensive items in the non-predictive short term discount period, due to they do not want to loss this large discount purchase price chance. So, short time discounted sale price, it is another method to persuade consumers to choose to buy the brand's any products in short time pressure consumption environment.

The another persuading time pressure consumption method is that it can let consumers to think more habitual buying the kind of products. products like stationery, groceries, food etc. fall under this category. For example, when the consumer fees the brand of any products ,he/she has habitual purchase experience, of he/she feels that the brand's any products won't sell in market temporary, even he/she can not buy it to use again. Then, it is possible to influence him/her to feel immediate purchase need to buy a lot of product or food number to keep to use or eat later in the time pressure environment, e.g. the food consumer buys the brand of any breads to eat in supermarkets habitually, but in this moth, he/she watchs TV advertisement to be acknowledge this brand of any breads won't be bought from any supermarkets as soon as possible. Hence, it is possible to influence him/her to plan to make choice to buy a lot of number of this brand of any breads in order to keep the enough of this brand of breads number to eat later. So, this brand of any breads sale loss in supermarkets that will cause the habitual food consumers of this brand of breads, whom make consumption choice to buy a lot number of this brands any breads in short time suddenly. Because they are eating this brand of any kinds of breads habitually. They feel much eating need to lot number of this brand of any breads in short period, because it can satisfy their habitual taste needs of this brand's any kinds of breads. So, brand loyalty and habitual consumption to the kind of product or food , which will result simply from the habit and it can influence the consumers feel consumption need to buy the brand's any kinds of products or foods when they feel that they may not buy it again or they can not earn discount advantage after the short time. So, any one of these sale strategies will have possible to raise the consumer individual consumption desire to the brand of products in the short time pressure consumption environment. Also it needs to spend much time to gather information in order to make purchase decision, because the brand had built confidence to consumers when they feel this brand's any products or foods are better to compare the similar brands' any products or foods habitually. So, time pressure consumption environment will persuade them to feel consumption desire to buy this brand's any products or foods in short time. When, they feel that they can not buy any more for this brand's any kinds of products or foods or discounting price in this final short purchase time.

In conclusion, these factors can influence consumer behaviors to be changed to feel time pressure need to do purchase decision making behavior from enough time gathering information available feeling behavior. They have these same views, e.g. habits and routines are very influential, particularly for behaviors repeated daily in a semi-automatic fashion. The consumer's past purchase experience to the brand's products, positive or negative emotion to the brand's products, and the brand's familiar, recognition are strong influence , the information available , it is the consumer's mind and the relative important information given to let the consumer knows form different advertisement medias matters for decision making, great between pieces of information and can be influenced by personal psychological timing limited pressure, the consumer's comparison to differences in price or other characteristics, many pursue value ( or in bargain), and compare to alternatives or past knowledge, consumer personal greater value on the immediate future and heavily discount future costs or savings to the brand of product, feeling simple and easy decision making process to the product , it can lead the consumer to avoid to spend long time to make purchasing decision and the consumer will easy to choose to buy the product when he/she feels have a loss value if he/she does not decide to buy the product in the short time. SO, it seems that when the marketer can motivate the consumer's consumption desire to feel saving money, promote health, avoid waste time and less nervous workload to gather information for comparison and evaluation alternatives aim. It is seen favorably by the consumer personal time pressure purchase decision making and sense of justice influence factors.

However, sociologists have categorised the motives for consumption behaviors in the short time by the fundamental consumption decision making needs or wants which they satisfy, e.g. having a clear understanding what benefits, characteristics, economic value to the brand's any products , feeling consumption decision making process is a leisure activity. These drivers for consumption behavior will either bring positive or negative to influence the consumer personal emotion, either owning enough time available or time pressure environmental impacts can be seen to influence whether the consumer feels he/she needs how long time to be spent to make comparison and evaluate alternatives in order to make final purchase choice in whom decision making process. Hence, the consumer himself/ herself time pressure consumption decision making feeling, it can bring positive purchase choice influence, when the marketer can build brand loyalty to let many consumers to feel in the market. Otherwise, if the marketer can not build brand loyalty to let many consumers to feel, but consumers feel time pressure to compare and evaluate its any products to other similar brands of products in the competitive market. Then, its products may be not the preference choices the many customers among the different brands of products choices. So, building long time brand loyalty relationship to satisfy consumers' needs, it will bring positive preference purchase choice to raise the sale effort to the brand of any products when consumers need to make purchase choice in time pressure consumption environment, e.g. seasonal discount sale period, products or foods shortage supply period, without any forever sale possibility in market. Hence , it seems that brand loyalty building factor will influence any brands of products /foods /service sale or provison number to be raised or reduced in possible. Also, it can explain why and how it has close cause and effect relationship between time pressure consumption environment and the brand loyalty building to the brand of products/foods/services to any marketers nowadays.

What are the in-store and out-store factors influence supermarket fast moving consumer decision

It is one interesting question: How can the brand of product seller influence the supermarket/store fast-moving consumers' more visual attention when the supermarket/store visitor is hurry to make decision to choose to buy which brand of product in time pressure environment? Supermarket/store fast-moving consumers do not usually spend much time to say in any supermarket shelf locations to choose numerous similar alternative brands of products. However, I assume the fast-moving supermarket/store consumer's decision is dependent on the interaction between the supermarket different shelf location sale environment and the mind of the consumer. So, the eye tracking explores this rapid processing that lacks conscious access or control to any supermarket or store consumers.

It brings this question: How product packing and placement ( as in-store factors) and recognition, preferences, and choice task ( as out-of-store factors) which will influence the supermarket / store consumer individual decision making process through visual attention. In split-second decision making, the ability to recognize and comprehend a brand of supermarket/ store product can significantly impact preferences. Hence, how the supermarket/store consumer's eye truly sees what whom mind is prepared to influence how much consumption desire to choose to buy the brand's product in short time decision making process when he/she stays in the shelf location, it has less than ten or more than ten different kinds of brands products or foods to let the visitor to choose in the supermarket or store.

Brand owners and product developers will feel responsibilities to overcome promotion or advertising or communication challenge in order to let consumers to know their products are launched on the market. However, it is not until the product reaches the supermarket shelf that has good quality to the effort is judged whether it has how much sale number every day in the supermarket. The judges are the consumers themselves how to make decision quickly through the personal time pressure environment with minor package information processing in the supermarket.

What does it take to be consider an option to influence the consumers' minds on visual attention in point-of-purchase decision making ? The supermarket's in-store activities and the consumer personal out-of-store activities will influence how his / her visual attention to the brand of products in the supermarket / store any shelf locations when he/she is walking to pass any shelf locations. So, it seems that any supermarkets or stores brands of products sale number , it has relation to every supermarket or store visitors' visual attention throughout the point to point ( shelf to shelf) decision making process in the supermarkets / stores. So, how much does the supermarket's visitors' time spending to obtain attention to the brand of produc? it will have possible to influence the brand of any products' sale number in the supermarket/store. Hence, in this limited timeframe, the consumer enters a decision making process that is in itself influenced by in-store and out-of-store both factors.

I shall explain what is supermarket / store space quality factor, e.g. top level versus floor level to different shelf variable height, weigh , or shelf space location factor as well as the product price elasticity and price-quality relationship to the brand of products both factors to influence every consumer decision making in supermarket/store. The in-store factor is more influential factor to compare out-of-store factor to influence consumers' decision in supermarket. For example, where the shampoo brand products are locating to be put on the shelf , it can influence the point to point behavior of shampoo product habitual buyers. If the buyer habitually chooses the shampoo brand products in the shelf location. Also, if all of the shampoo brand products are moved to another shelf locations to display its different kinds of shampoo products to cause the habitual buyer needs to spend much extra time to find where the another new shelf location is displaying the brand's shampoo products.

In this situation, information processing has a heightened decision making role as the buyer needs to spend much time to find where the brand's displayed shampoo products' shelf location to make non-habitual decision making between options. For habitual decisions, the consumer's visual attention is reduced to measuring visual search. However, when the brands of any shampoo products are moved to another new shelf location to display its different kinds of shampoo products. So, the act of another shelf new location search , it will influence the habitual shampoo buyer's visual attention to consider the brand of any shampoo products which are usually used to wash to his/her hair habitually. When he / she can find the other new brands of shampoo products are displayed on the old shelf displayed location of the brand of shampoo products. Hence, the traditional shelf displayed location to the brand of products, when the brand of products are moved to another new displayed shelf locations. This in-store factors that will influence traditional consumers through visual attention concerns to this brand of products more or less.

So, supermarket traditional shelf displayed variable location to the brand of products factor, which will have influence to the traditional consumers' visual attention to do either buying the brand's products or buying another brand's products to replace it, when the traditional consumer feels difficult that he/she needs to spend extra longer time to find whether where is the traditional useful product's displayed shelf location. Then, it will be possible to influence the traditional consumer's traditional purchase decision to the brand's product, and he/she will choose to buy another brand of product to replace when it can be displayed to the shelf location to attract the consumer's visual attention more.

It is one important in-store shelf displayed factor to influence the traditional fast-moving consumer individual purchase decision making behavioral change in any supermarkets or stores when they feel hurry to do personal time pressure consumption decision to make purchase final decision in the point to point counter purchase ( the brand's of products are moved from the traditional shelf location visual attention moves to the strange shelf location visual attention) in supermarket time pressure consumption environment.

Hence, in supermarket time pressure consumption environment, in -store and out-of-sore both factors can influence fast-moving consumer individual purchase decision making. The in-store factors can influence product packaging, product placement components as well as the out-store factors can influence choice task, preference and brand recognition components. So, it is common to influence supermarket consumers choose do personal time pressure purchase consumption decision of visual attention purchase behaviors. The different brands' products are displayed to different shelf locations in order to cause shelf displaying products' different decision making effect.

However, instead of shelf displaying location factor, package will also influence consumers' decision making, due to the influence of minute differences in packaging design on visual attention. When, the supermarket consumer feels the brands are not familiar or unfamiliar. Then, he/she will spend more time to evaluate and verify the unfamiliar brands' products whether which one is value to buy in her/his decision making process. He/she will feel visual attention need in order to evaluate in set of brand alternatives to make conscious demand mind cognitive effort by involving working memory. So, if the product's package is attractive, even the consumer is unfamiliar the brand's any product choices which are displayed on the shelf location in the supermarket. The brand's attractive package factor can influence the consumer to raise whom visual attention. Then, the attractive package factor can increase much visual attention chance to many consumers when they are walking to pass through the unfamiliar brand's any products' shelf displaying location considerably. So, it explains when attractive package factor may solve the visual attention problem to fast-moving consumers when they are visiting one strange supermarket to find anywhere unfamiliar brand's products' shelf displaying locations. Because they are the non-traditional consumers to the unfamiliar brand's products, they won't be influenced to choose either buying or not buying the unfamiliar brand's products. When the unfamiliar brand's products are moved to another new shelf displayed location. So, if the unfamiliar brand has attractive package to let the non-traditional consumers feel visual attention when they are passing through the strange shelf displayed location. Then, it can raise purchase chance to the non-traditional consumers target number when they are staying in the strange supermarket. In conclusion, the brand of products' shelf displaying location and package factors may bring much influence to any traditional or non-traditional consumer behaviors in supermarket or store time pressure consumption environment.

What consumption is most
influenced in preference choice
by time pressure

What kinds of services or products are most influenced to consumer behavioral change by time pressure? Can time pressure factor influence more preference to other factors, such as age, culture, income level, habitual shopping, family or friend relationship etc. factors to influence consumer behavioral choice to these kinds of services or products in consumption market? I shall indicate some kinds of services or products consumption models to explain how time pressure can influence consumers to choose to consume its services or buy its products.

Firstly, for theme park entertainment industry example, has it time pressure to cause any theme park visitors, e.g. Walt Disney entertainment theme park to influence them to feel time pressure to enjoy their emotions to play any entertainment machine facilities and it brings negative emotion to choose the entertainment theme park entertainment consumption activities.

For Walt Disney entertainment theme park example, every visitor needs to pay a fixed ticket fee to enter Disney theme park. So, however, he/she chooses to play how many number of entertainment activities facilities, e.g. only one entertainment playing facility, or more than one entertainment playing facilities. The Disney visitor needs to pay the same ticket fee to enter Disney. So, it will cause the visitors feel unfair , they do not choose to play any entertainment facilities or play only less number of entertainment facilities. Because they need to pay the same ticket price to same to the visitors, who choose to play many entertainment facilities number in Disney. So, it brings this question: Does the Disney visitor feel time pressure when he/she chooses to play many number of entertainment facilities , but he/she will not enjoy to carry on other activities in Disney, e.g. shopping, visiting cinema to watch movies, walking around the whole Disney anywhere to view scene activities. Because US Disney entertainment theme park is very large . It has not only entertainment facilities to attract visitors to play. It has many places are value to visitors to visit or enjoy the other free charge entertainment activities , such as visiting Disney gardens, visiting ocean park, visiting Disney cinema to watch free movies, view scene or seeing free charge ocean animal performance shows , going to Disney shopping centers to shopping, visiting Disney library to read books, visiting Disney ocean park to view different kinds of beautiful fishes non-entertainment machine facility playing activities. All of these activities are value to any Disney visitors to choose to play or visit, instead of entertainment machine facilities activities. So, if one visitor hopes only to spend one day in US Walt Disney entertainment theme park. He/she will feel hurry to choose to play any machine entertainment facilities, or he/she won't choose any machine entertainment facilities to play in Disney because he/she also hopes to play other non-machine entertainment facilities activities, e.g. visiting garden, visiting ocean park, visiting library, visiting cinema to watch free movies, visiting garden to play free charge boats water entertainment activities, watching ocean animal show performance etc. different kinds of entertainment activities, even walking around anywhere fun and excite places in Disney theme park. Hence, the Disney visitor will feel time pressure to choose either playing any kinds of entertainment machine facilities or visiting different places in the whole one day in Disney.

Hence, time pressure factor may influence any one of Disney visitors how to choose any entertainment activities to spend time in Disney. It will bring this question: Because the Disney ticket price is fixed fee, can the Disney visitor will feel unfair to cause negative emotion, if the Disney visitor feels time pressure to choose to play any kinds of machine entertainment activities or doing other non-machine entertainment activities in the Disney visitor's limited timeframe, during he/she stays in Disney? So, it seems that time pressure psychological factor will may influence some Disney visitors to feel unhappy, negative emotion, when they feel their entertainment activities choices are wrong or doing wring entertainment decision making in his/her limited timeframe. Consequently, time pressure factor will influence some feeling time pressure Disney visitors won't choose to enter Disney again. Hence, time pressure factor can have much influence to theme park visitors' behavioral change, instead of whether the entertainment theme park's machine entertainment facilities are attractive or enjoyable playing or how many entertainment facilities are supplied to let visitors to play in the entertainment theme park. So, entertainment theme park service provide need to consider whether their ticket prices are reasonable to let visitors feel, if they do not want to reduce theme park visitors number seriously.

The another example is restaurant food service industry. Can time pressure influence food consumers to choose the restaurant to eat? Instead of food taste, price, seats available providing, restaurant location, public transportation facilities available etc. factors, which can influence the food consumer individual choice to the restaurant.

Is time pressure another one main factor to influence food consumers choice to the restaurant? In what situation, food consumers will feel time pressure to influence whose preference restaurant choice? I assume that the restaurant 's price is reasonable, public transportation facility is convenient to catch to go to the restaurant, food taste is acceptable to the food consumer. Although all above these factors are accepted to the food consumer . But when the food consumer feels hurry to hope to find one restaurant to eat and he/she hopes to spend less time to sit down to eat in the restaurant , e.g. less than one hour. Then, the food consumer will compare all the restaurants are near to whose working place or school , if he/she is one student or one working person. Because he/she needs to eat lunch to go to school or go to office to work. So, the restaurant's food taste, price is not the main factor to influence him/her to choose to eat.

Otherwise, whether the restaurant needs him/her to spend how long queue time to wait, or/and the restaurant needs how long cooking time to let him/her to eat, the restaurant needs him/her to walk how long time to arrive the restaurant. All of these factors concern " efficient cooking time, queue waiting time service performance" issues to the restaurant, which are the main evaluation requirements to influence the feeling time pressure food consumer to make decision whether he/she either still ought follow the better food taste, cheap food price factors to be preference decision or he/she ought follow short time queue time waiting or without queue time waiting, fast cooking waiting time factors to be preference restaurant consumption decision.

Hence, it seems that a feeling time pressure food consumer, he/she ought choose the restaurant to eat in preference when it does not need him/her to wait long queue time and wait long cooking time. Otherwise, when the food consumer does not feel hurry to eat, he/she ought choose the restaurant, it can provide good taste food, cheap price in preference to eat.

Hence, time pressure personal feeling will influence students or working people food consumers' preference restaurant choice when the restaurant can provide short time queue waiting or without queue waiting and fast cooking time service preference to satisfy their needs.

However , in some situation, time pressure can influence consumers to choose the service, even its price is expensive than other services. For example, public transportation tool choices service. When one passenger has need to find one kind public transportation tool to catch from the place to another destination, but the destination is far away from his/her location. He/she hopes to catch the kind of public transportation tool to arrive the destination about one hour. Although, his/her location has cheap public transportation tools to choose, e.g. bus, train, tram, ferry, underground train. But, he/she feels that all of these public transportation tools need to spend longer time to compare taxi to arrive the destination. Although, these public transportation tools can be possible to arrive the destination with one house and they must charge cheaper fee to compare taxi. But, however the passenger hopes to arrive the destination in the shortest time. The most important influential factor is that the passenger feels personal time pressure to need to arrive the destination fast and taxi public transportation tool is believed the fast transportation tool to arrive any destination to compare other general public transportation tools , when it has no traffic jam external environment factor influence. So, time pressure factor will influence passenger to choose taxi transportation tool in preference. Also, it seems that when the place often has many time pressure passengers are living. Then, the place's taxi business will be possible better than other locations. Hence, it implies that time pressure factor will bring need or demand number to be increased to some services.

Time pressure also influences how consumers choose to buy the kind of product, when he/she feels that the kind of product will be old fashion or it is not popular to use in society. For example, computer product, the traditional desktop large heavy weight computers will be possible to be replaced to use at home or office or any building places. Due to the laptop small light weight computers , it can be brought to anywhere by the users easily, even it can be brought to catch public transportation tool to use, it can be brought to restaurant, library, shopping center etc. different public places to use conveniently. Due to some working people feel hurry to use computer to do their tasks, e.g. typing one document in short time. If they are not working in office and they have no computer on hand. They will worry about that they can not finish their tasks to give their bosses in limited time on the working day.

Hence, laptop computer will be one good chocie of task tool for busy working people when they need to often to use computer to finish urgent tasks in any time. Hence, it seems that the feeling time pressure working people will choose laptop computer in preference more than desktop traditional computer working tool. Due to the feeling time pressure workers, they feel that they can not finish their daily tasks in office. So, they will feel to need to use laptop computer task tool to help them to do office tasks . When they are catching transportation tool to go home or office time or lunch time , or holiday time. So, laptop computer product is more popular to time pressure working people target consumers.

Laptop computer products can also increase the feeling time pressure student consumers' needs. Because when one students feel home time is not enough to use computer to do their homeworkers at homes. When some students finish all lessons in schools and they need to catch public transportation tools to go home, in this catching public transportation time, they will be possible to hope to use one laptop computer to do their homework. So, one student who often feels time pressure to do whose homework, he will feel need to buy one laptop to carry it to anywhere, e.g. library, garden, school etc. different places. Then, he/she can do whom housework at any places in any time conveniently. Hence, it seems that their laptop computer products will be time pressure consumers' preference task tool.

In conclusion, the different factors influence consumer behaviors. Time pressure factor may be one main factor to influence consumers to choose to buy the kind of product or consume the kind of service in preference. So, when th consumer feels time pressure to influence him/her to do preference choice to consume the kind of service of buy the kind of product. It is possible to occur to influence he/she does irrational economic choice decision. Hence, time pressure factor can being positive or negative both consumption emotion to some kinds of services or products . Hence, the increasing or decreasing number of consumers to some kinds of products or services, it has absolute relationship between of them. So, any product sellers or service providers can not neglect the importance of how time pressure factor influences consumer behavior in our nowadays society.

Time pressure impacts consumer
behavioral effect

I shall indicate cases to explain that how time pressure environment factor impacts consumer behavior as well as what effects will be brought by time pressure consumer behavioral cause. Instead of above discussions concern how customer personal time pressure psychological factor influence, whether hoe time pressure environment factor will also influence consumer behavior. What are the difference between time pressure environment factor and time pressure consumer personal psychological factor? I shall explain as below:

Firstly, the impact of life satisfaction is caused by time pressure on consumers responses. Can effective advertising can impact of life satisfaction when the consumer feels need to buy the kind of product in any time pressure environment? Can effective advertising bring direct impact on sales when the consumer feels need to buy the kind of product in time pressure environment? Effective advertising may being advantages, includes customers feel easy to accept of price increases, favorable publicity, and reshaping market segmentation.

However, when the customer feels need life satisfaction in time pressure lif environment. The time pressure life environment ought impact on the consumer responses on advertising. Hence, when the consumer needs to live in the time pressure life environment. The over-commercialization of advertising ought impact the consumer chooses to buy the brand of product, when the seller has attractive advertising to bring purchase incentives to influence consumption desire to the time pressure environment influential consumer. For example, when the summer season will change to winter season, the ice cream consumers begins to feel weather will change to cold weather. Because many people feel more cold in the beginning. This is seasonable time pressure environment feeling, it may influence many ice-cream likers feel ice-cream may be possible shortage in hot weather or summer season, due to many ice-creams will be bought in summer weather to cause supermarkets in possible. So, if the brand ice-cream can make attractive advertisement to persuade ice-in cream number will be reduced in the coming winter season beginning. So, it may influence many ice-cream likers choose to buy this brand's ice-cream in preference in summer. Because they feel fear none of any this brand's ice-creams can be sold in supermarkets in summer. Because they feel this brand's ice-cream , it's problem to let they can buy any different kinds of ice-cream taste to eat from any supermarkets in summer season. Hence, it explains why effective or attractive advertising may increase sale number, when consumers feel the brand's product number will be shortage or reduced from the seasonal time pressure external environment factor influence.

Secondly, I shall discuss what is the relationship between the effects of product popularity and time pressure on consumer responses? When a brand is popular to let many customers to familiarize in society. Does it increase time pressure to influence consumers choose in preference? Time pressure remaining to product popularity concerns how much sale number is raised to persuade consumers to choose to buy a preference for ecommerce online shopping. It seems to be one time pressure online sale environment. The effects of the ecommerce online shopping environment has relationship between pressure and product popularity on perceived risk and purchase intention.

In ecommerce online sale environment time pressure is operation at the time remaining for consumers to sign up the online seller' website and property popularity is operation to the number of products already sold at the moment when consumers visit the web page. Hence, when on online consumer has intention to buy any products from internet. He/she will attempt to type the product name, then he/she will find some webpages which can provide the different brands of product photos, their prices information to let the consumer to compare whether which brand of product price is more reasonable, better quality , good product image from the web pages' advertisement information to let him/her to evaluate. Hence, any product web page will influence how every online customer feeling is good or bad to the web page's any brands of products. If the consumer feel the web page has many high product popularity indicators, it may bring a high consumption desire to let the online customer to evaluate the web page all products in order to compare which brand of product is the best to choose to buy in time webpage view pressure consumption environment. Otherwise, if the consumer feels the web page has high product popularity indicator , it may bring a less consumption desire to let the online consumer to evaluate any of the webpage products to choose to buy. So, online webpage advertising information will be one time pressure online ecommerce consumption environment.

I assume that online shopping consumers won't like to stay to view on any webpage long time. It is possible that they choose to click more web pages to hope to find more different familiar and unfamiliar both brands of products information in order to make more accurate comparison and evaluation from more different kinds of brands of products in order to make the most accurate online shopping decision. Hence, any brands of products online webpage information will be one time pressure limited sale environment to consumers feel that they need to make the most accurate online purchase decision in short time. Moreover, it seems that if the brand of products which can be showed on the popular product webpage, the it will have much sale chance to let online purchasers familiarize in order to increase sale opportunity more easily.

Finally, I shall explain what is the meaning of external time pressure consumption environment is the long time queue waiting consumption environment. I shall explain how to achieve one simplistic queueing system to solve long time queue waiting problem to bring consumers' negative emotion influence to choose to consume the service or buy the product in preference.

For entertainment service example, e.g. queueing at the cinema counter to buy one ticket to watch the movie , or queueing at the music hall to buy one ticket to listen the music performance show activities. The audiences' ticket purchase aims to sit down in the cinema or music hall to enjoy to listen and see pretty music performance or watch the attractive movie comfortable within one to two hours entertainment time. If the movie or music performance show is attractive, the cinema or music hall will have many audiences accept to spend long time to queue to buy the ticket.

However, if the cinema or music hall needs audience consumers to queue long time to buy the ticket, e.g. one house , even more than one house queueing time to wait to buy the ticket to watch the movie or listen the music performance show. Then, the long time queue waiting problem will be possible to cause a lot audiences number to be reduced, because they feel that they need to spend much time pressure to queue to by the ticket to listen the music performance show or watch the movie.

However, of these unacceptable too long queue time audiences can have another/ other cinema(s), music hall(s) to buy the same price , even more low price of movie ticket or music performance show ticket in short time. Then, they must leave the present cinema queue and go to the another cinema or music hall to buy ticket to watch the same movie or listen the same music performance show. So, long time queue is one external time pressure environment to influence consumer's preference choice to the service provider, when they feel it has another service provider does not need them or these audiences need to spend same long time queue time to wait to buy the ticket in order to enjoy the service, e.g. listening music performance show, watching movie.

Hence, in a high time pressure queue situation where decision makers, e.g. audiences have less time than needed ( or perceived needed). It is ·very likely that they feel the queue waiting time stress of copying with themselves queue waiting time maximum limitation. So, if the movie ticket purchase audience feels that he/she will need to spend more than half hour to queue and half hour is himself/herself the maximum acceptable queue time level. So, his/her queue long time pressuree negative emotion feeling will influence him/her to leave the cinema to choose another cinema. He/ she feels that ir does not need him/her to queue more than half hour in order to buy the ticket to watch the same movie in the another cinema, he/she can feel more comfortable to watch the movie. So, long time queue will influence some audiences choose another service provider to replace it in possible short time, when they feel waiting in a queue is irritating, frustrating and hence costly.

What is a simplistic queueing system and how it can solve above queue problem. For a grocery store queueing counter case example, for one Apply brand computer shop example, the day's most busy queue time , there are about between fifty and hundred Apply brand potential computer buyers numbers every hour in the day. They need to queue to enquire the salespeople concern to any useful opinions to let them to know in order to make purchase decisions. But, the Apple brand computer shop lacks enough salespeople to answer their enquiries concern any computer purchase challenges. Every computer enquiry potential purchaser needs to spend at least half hour , even more time to queue to wait the salesperson to answer his/her enquiry in the counter queueing line. Hence, the feeling long time queue enquiry waiting consumers will feel time pressure to queue. Then, they will choose to leave the Apple brand computer shop's counter queue line. Consequently, the Apple brand computer will lose many potential computer buyers on the busy day.

The most simple solution is that it can increase the salespeople number in the most busy enquiry time every day. Hence, when every computer potential enquiry customer can contact every salesperson to listen whom opinion concerns his/her any computer enquiry issues in order to let he/she feels that they every one can provide excellent sale service computer issues enquiry explanation performance to satisfy his/her enquiry need to let himself/herself to feel in the short enquiry time. Due to they do not need to spend long queue time to wait every salesperson's feedback or opinion to solve their enquiries in the computer shop. Because they do not feel pressure to spend long time to queue to wait the computer shops every salesperson's opinion. So, they will raise satisfactory feeling to the Apple computer shop's every salesperson individual sale enquiry service performance.

Consequently, the day's computer sale number will be possible to raise after the salespeople can spend much time to solve their enquiries effectively and efficiently.

● The reasons cause consumers feel
time pressure

What factors can cause consumers feel time pressure to but the product in the personal time limited dominated consumption environment? It is one interesting question: Why does the consumer feel time pressure to make short time purchase decision making? I shall indicate some cases to explain this possibility as below:

First, I shall indicate household purchaser time pressure consumption behavior. Consumer house buyer behavior, some house buyer will feel personal time pressure to choose the different houses to make house purchase decision in short time. For example, if the house developer has a 30% discount house price to sell only in the short three months. So, after this three months, all house purchaser will need to pay the original house price. If the house developer's houses prices are between US dollar one million to two million every house. For one million house price after 30% discount , the house buyer only needs to pay seventy million. For two million house price after 30 % discount, the house buyer only needs to pay one hundred and fouty million. So, expensive product's financing factor will influence the buyer's consumption time pressure, such as the house discount price case, due to the house developer's houses prices are very expensive. However, if any house buyers can make decision to buy its houses in three months. Then, they can pay les 30% of the houses prices. Such as the original price one million house, the house buyer can pay less thirty million amount or the original price two million houses prices. The house buyer can pay less sixty million amount. So, the large discount financing amount may be attractive purchase method to influence many house buyers feel time pressure to decide whether they ought choose to buy the property developer's houses in these three months. It is one short term cheap house financing price to let many house buyers feel time pressure to make house purchase decision from this house developer in these three months . Hence, short term high discount price to expensive product financing factor will influence consumers feel it is right time to make pressure consumption decision.

Hence, such as this three months house discount price case, when the property buyer gain this property developer's knowledge of three months house discount price message. This sudden three months house discount price message will be one attractive knowledge of factor to impact the potential property buyers' house purchase desires to be raised in three months time pressure house purchase consumption environment. So, it is one feeling sudden time pressure consumption desire good example for this three months large discount attractive houses price to influence house buyers to make house purchase decision from the house developer in these three months. Consequently, house developer will have possible to raise the large house sale number , if this 30 % house discount price can let many property buyers feel it is one worth purchase price in these three months. So, they will consider that they can not pay less 30% discount price to buy this house developer's any houses after three months. So they need to make house purchase decision in these three months short term time pressure house consumption market for this property developer.

So, this time pressure financing advantage will only bring benefit to this property developer, this time pressure financing advantage won't bring benefit to other property developers, because all property buyers feel need to make property purchase decision in these three months suddenly, due to this property developer can provide a special 30 discount price to any property final decision making to choose to buy its houses in these three months temporary short time. It seems that three months short time can cause final house purchase choice time pressure to any potential property buyers. They expect to gain high discount price to buy any expensive houses. So, these expensive house potential buyers will feel need to make final expensive house purchase decision to choose to buy this property developer's expensive houses in these final three months period. So, time pressure can occur in any short period, when the seller can provide any special sale promotion to persuade consumers to feel need to make sudden time pressure that purchase decision is they hope to earn special sale promotion consumption in the short limited sale period for the seller.

Hence, consumer personal time pressure feeling, it can be predictive to any time occurrence psychological consumption, feeling, such as the property developer's sudden high per cent discount price to expensive house less burden factor to influence the expensive house buyers feel that whether they ought do choice house purchase decision in these short term three months , because the house developer's non predictive and sudden attractive expensive houses reducing prices strategy. So, this property developer's short term three months high house discount price time pressure consumption strategy may persuade or attract , even encourage many potential expensive house buyers choose to spend lesser amount to buy this property developer's discount houses, either is paid by house mortgage bank loan lending payment method or installment payment method or on-time all payment method. So, the different house payment choice buyers will be influenced to make immediate property purchase decision in these three months time pressure period from this property developer's expensive discounted house number influence.

However, in this house market time pressure consumption environment, the property developer's expensive house supply number may also have influential effort to excite the expensive house buyers' house purchase consumption desires, for example, if the other expensive house property developers' between US one million and US two million of every property price's these houses in the country's property marker total supply number is one thousand property unit number. The potential property buyers , they plan to buy these amounts of expensive houses , the property buyers estimate three thousand buyers number at least. Hence, it seems that these expensive house buyers' demand id more than three times to expensive property supply number.

Moreover, the other property developer's expensive property developers ' expensive house prices have no any discount in this three months periods, and some property developers' expensive house prices tend to increase 1 to 10 per cent in these three months period. Hence if the property developer can supply at least three thousand property units number between US one million and US two million sale price and all of these expensive houses are reduced 30 per cent discount to sell in these three months .

Consequently, it is possible to persuade all estimated three thousand expensive house potential buyers choose to buy this property developer's houses in these three months in possible. So, it explain that why this property developer's expensive discounted house supply number will influence these property buyers' preference choice. If this property developer has only one thousand expensive houses to be supplied by discounted 30% sale price. Then, it will cause shortage of expensive houses to satisfy these three thousand expensive house buyer estimated number in the country in three month discount sale promotion period.

Consequently, this property developer will lose two thousand these prices of expensive house potential buyers number in all these three months discounted sale period . I assume that all these three thousand expensive house property buyers will be influenced to make choice to buy its all discounted expensive houses in these three month time pressure discounted sale period. So, it needs to do data gather concerns how many of thee expensive house potential house buyers number in its country in order to avoid discounted expensive houses supply number to cause shortage supply challenges and bring these expensive house potential buyers lose number in these three months period.

In conclusion, it explains why that supply number will influence this property developer's sale number in these three months sale period. Consequently, time pressure sale strategy and supply number has close relationship to influence the seller's sale number in the time pressure sale period.

Secondly, I shall discuss how does environment time pressure factor influences consumer behavior? Does time pressure influence consumer donating behavior? I assume that external environment time pressure factor can influence consumer changes whom original purchase decision making. What circumstance's time can influence consumer individual to feel time pressure to consume. For example, when the consumer expects have one hour to choose whether which brand of product to buy among the different kinds of products. The circumstance is changed suddenly. It influences the consumers feel that they has only 10 minutes to make the final purchase decision.

Why does the consumer feel enough brand of product? What external circumstance factors influence he/she feels only 10 minutes time to make the final purchase decision suddenly? For travel fair time limited external environment influential pressure travelling consumption case example, the international travel fair can indicate that time limited pressure has positive significant influence on traveler perceived value and purchase intention in short time. In addition, perceived value is served as a mediating factor between the relationship of time limited pressure and feeling travelling entertainment purchase intention to the travel fair visitors. It has a beneficial reference for planning a travelling show or fair marketing strategy.

One attractive travelling fair/show can promote the country's different attractive travelling destinations to let the travelling show's visitors to know. It can particularly influence the visitors' long time travelling planning , it can be shorten be short time travelling planning, e.g. after one year's travelling planning can be influenced to make immediate focused on choosing the country's travelling decision if he/she feels the country has more attractive travelling destinations, he/she prefers to go to travel in short time, e.g. within 6 months . So, when the travelling exhibition fair/ show can provide the country's beautiful scene photos to let the visitors to view. Then, it will bring effective time pressure feeling to let some travelling visitors feel travelling needs immediately in the travelling exhibition show/ fair . This travelling exhibition show/fair can bring the time limited pressure benefit. It is as an external environment factor that can influence the travelling visitors' travelling desires to be raised , when they can view many beneficial scene photos of the country' different undiscovered travelling destination . Then, it can increase their travelling desires to the country in possible.

I shall explain why travelling exhibition show/fair can play an important role in travelling consumer perceived quality and travelling country destination choice decision making to influence travelling visitors feel time limited pressure. However, perceived value has been show to be a value has been shown to be a value of perceived quality and perceived sacrifice to cause travelling visitors feel more interesting to choose to travel the country when they can view the attractive beautiful scene photos in the travelling exhibition show/fair.

A successful travelling exhibition show/fair can bring time limited process increases , the travelling visitors pay more attention to key travelling destination features and positive travelling information from the scene photos and travelling destinations introduction. So , the country's attractive travelling destinations scene photos and clear travelling introduction to different destinations information will be important message to let the different countries' travelling visitors to know when they spend a limited time to enter the travelling exhibition show/fair to view the different scene photos . If the travelling visitor feel very satisfied to the country's travelling exhibition show/fair. Then, this travelling exhibition excite whom travelling interest to choose to go to the country to travel in short time, when the travelling visitors are influenced to feel the country has many beautiful destinations where they feel have travelling interest in the limited time pressure travelling exhibition show/fair environment. If the travelling exhibition show/fair needs they to pay enter fee and it has only two hours or less time to permit to stay in the travelling exhibition show/fair.

Hence, if the time pressure limited travelling exhibition show/fair can let the travelling visitors feel attractive and enjoyable view feeling when they look every the country's any scene beautiful photos and indication how to the different travelling destinations and explains why the country's travelling places are value travelling destinations to let the exhibition visitors to know, when they do not know or discover these any one of value travelling places in the country before. Then, this limited time staying travelling exhibition show/fair will bring positive time pressure to influence some travelling visitors feel interesting to visit the country's unknown or discovery travelling destinations in short time. So, all attractive travelling exhibition shows/fairs are one external environment time limited positive pressure factor to excite some travelling visitors' travelling desires in short time in possible.

Instead of travelling exhibition show/fair can bring external environment positive limited time positive pressure to excite travelling visitors' travelling consumption desires, the another external environment positive limited time positive pressure case is that mobile coupons of limited mobile phone sale number or discount mobile phone call payment plan in short time case. How and why mobile coupons can excite any mobile consumption and/ or mobile phone call user choice to the mobile phone sale company or mobile phone call service provider.

An effective mobile plane useful limited time beneficial purchase strategy can encourage some mobile phone consumers to choose to use the brand mobile useful phone call service plan immediate if the mobile phone call service plan is attractive to the mobile phone call consumer . For example, dynamic discounts strategies are used by marketers to send scarce message which lead to higher consumers' mobile phone purchase intention. An utility increasing discount strategy provides mobile phone call users with an increasing discount over time ( e.g. 30% discount for in-store consumption for 30 minutes, after which the discount increases to 40 % , an utility discount strategy provides the same discounts for mobile phone call users over a specific promotional period ( e.g. 40% discount from 9AM to 5 PM) phone call using time. An utility decreasing discount strategy offers mobile phone call users with a decreasing discount over time ( e.g. 40% discount for in -store consumption for 10 minutes, after which the discount decreases to 30%).

However, these three different discount strategies for bargaining have different impacts on outcomes. However, they have same influences to lead mobile phone call users feel time pressure to do choose whether this mobile phone call using plan is suitable. If the mobile phone call user feels this mobile phone call using plan is suitable to use, then this mobile coupon promotion strategy can influence mobile phone user feels limited time pressure to persuade him/her to choose to use its mobile phone call service under different time limitation, quantity limitation and discount strategies on the mobile phone user's mobile phone call plan using intention.

Furthermore, I hypothesize that the brand of mobile phone quantity, limited scarcity message that gives a perception that the brand of any kinds of mobile phones are limited for purchase, it will have a positive impact on mobile phone consumers' perceived value of mobile products, leading to a greater tend to make mobile phone purchase decision immediately. Hence, mobile coupon is one type of price-incentive promotion. In various price incentives, discount strategy is a mode of price negotiation between the mobile product consumer and the merchant, such as the mobile phone seller , mobile phone call user and mobile phone call service provider.

However, mobile coupons offer discount under a time constraint to induce perceived scarcity. Scarce commodities are more attractive than those with plenty inventory due to the in special and uniqueness of the former perceived by the consumer. However, scarcity has both forms. They include quantity scarce can let consumers feel need to buy the product in short time. Otherwise, due to stock shortage or low inventory to influence they can not brought the kind of product. Time scarcity means products are for sale only for a designated

May time dominate consumption
final purchase decision making

Whether can time limited pressure dominate consumer individual to make more rational purchase decision? Can the consumer make more rational decision , when he/she has enough time to make final purchase decision? I shall explain why and how the consumer can make more rational decision when he/she has enough time as well as I shall explain that without time pressure environment. It may dominate consumers to make more rational or more accurate decision making.

I assume that it is the final time limited pressure day to nee the consumer to spend more nervous do time final purchase decision among the different kinds of similar products choices, e.g. air conditions . If the consumer decides that the day is the final purchase decision to choose to buy one air condition among these different brands of similar air conditions in the super store. So, if on the that day, he/she can not make any final decision to choose which brand of air condition to buy on that final consumption day in the super store when the super store visitor sees the final air condition consumption day advertisement in this year in this super store . Then, he/she won't buy any air condition again if he/she can not buy on that day in this super store.

The another time dominates immediate purchase behavior is that I assume that one common air condition can not be bought in short time later if all air condition consumers can not make decision to buy any air condition in this super store. So, his/her personal time limited pressure can dominate whose final or condition purchase decision in this super store on that day. If the store has many different brands of air conditions to lead him/her to spend long time to compare which is th best worth to buy in this super store. Then, it will let him/her to feel difficult to make the air condition final purchase decision in the store on that day. Otherwise, if the super store has less different brands of air conditions to need him/her to spend less time to compare which is the best worth to buy in the store. Then, he/she may make the final air condition purchase decision making more easily on that day.

So, the final air condition purchase day of the super store, the super store's air condition final day's time can dominate the air condition buyer to make air condition purchase decision immediately. Due to he/she feels that all of these day brands air conditions can not bought from this super store after that day. So, he/she needs to make the air condition purchase decision making in this super store on that final air condition purchase day in this year. Because it is the final air condition purchase day in this super store of all sir conditions products. If he/she can not make the choice to buy any one brand of air condition in this store. Then, it is possible that he/she will lose this store's final cheap price air condition purchase benefits. However, if this super store has too many brands of air conditions need him/her to choose. It will cause him/her to spend more time to choose. Consequently, it will cause he/she feels difficult to compare which brand of air condition is the best and he / she does not choose to buy any one in this super store.

Hence, this super store ought have less number different brands of air conditions to let every air condition consumer to choose in order to let they can make final air condition purchase decision on this air condition cheap price purchase final day. So, less different number brands of air conditions will dominate the consumers to spend less time to make purchase decision immediately and easily on that final sale day in this super store. Hence, it seems that the super store's final air conditions sold day time will dominate many air condition visitors to make purchase decision when they visit this super store in summer season on that day in this super store. Because all this super store's air condition consumers do not expect that they can not buy the best quality of air condition in this super store final sold day , due to air condition stocks number shorten challenge is not supplied enough on that final cheap purchase day in this super store. Consequently, that time pressure will increase to influence them to make the final air condition purchase decision in the final sold day' s short time, before this super store closing time on that day. Their time pressure feeling comes from the super store 's air condition number shortage supply in possibility. It will dominate them to make the final air condition purchase decision in this super store in short time.

The another time dominates immediate purchase behavior case is that I assume that one common picture painter( actor), he finds one architect to help him to build one house. The architect only needs to follow his house picture to build one house. The common picture painter tells him that he will give him building expenditure and building profit after he helps him to build the house profit after he helps him to build the house successfully. After six months, the architect made one decision, he did not demand the famous picture painter paid him for the building service fee. But, he needed him give the house picture to him to replace the building service fee. Because the picture painter feels that he didn't need to pay the building service fee to him to buy the architect's building service in these six months building time. Hence, he accepted his offer to give his common house picture to the architect for his reward.

I assume that this six months time dominate the architect to make the final building service fee decision either acceptance the common picture painter customer's building service fee or acceptance his common house picture replaces the building service fee. However, the architect believes that this common house picture can have higher selling price to compare his building service fee income. Consequently, I assume that his evaluation is right, this house picture selling price is more than three times to compare his past six months' building service income. So, it proved that his choice is right, because he could earn more than three times of his building service income after he decided to accept the common picture painter's this house picture to attempt to sell it in the picture auction market. It seems that this six months long house building time can dominate these both buyer and seller's purchase and selling behaviors, such as this picture painter and this architect. When the architect has this six months enough time to let the picture painter to change his building service offer decision from building service fee payment to his common house picture offer exchange. This architect can achieve his intention to let him to accept his free house picture sold product exchange offer more easily. Otherwise, if the architect can not need six months to build this house, he only needs three months or less time to build this house, then it is possible that the picture painter won't accept his this house picture offer to replace his building service fee easily. If he considers that whether his this house picture's selling price has possible to sell higher price to compare this building service fee for this house picture. He will choose to sell this house picture himself. Hence, due to the picture painter can not sell this house picture in this past six months. So, in this six months period, the house painter can not sell this house picture in picture auction market. This six months period can dominate his low market worth selling feeling to this house picture as well as it can influence him to make this house picture exchange decision to replace his house service fee.

The picture painter will ask himself, ought the house picture painter need to wait how long time to sell this picture in auction market, because he does not know whether the architect needs how long time to build this house? So, this house building time can dominate the picture painter's acceptance of the architect's this free house picture product exchange offer, which is easier acceptance or difficult acceptance . In this six month' house building period between the architect service provider and the picture painter house buyer. Hence, the house building time can dominate the house building provider and the picture painter's house building buyer both house picture free exchange purchase change behavioral choice between of them influentially.

The another time dominates consumption behavior case is that time rich or time poor factor, e.g. one fast food famous restaurant , its success is not only due to its fast food good taste factor, its restaurant location whether is close to the time poor people's offices, it is one main factor. Because this fast food famous restaurant only choose to build its restaurants to close to offices in any large cities in different countries. Hence, the franchisees need to pay expensive franchise loyalty income to buy its franchise in order to it can supply fast foods to the franchisees to sell, but they also need to pay expensive rent to this fast food franchiser, due to their fast food restaurant locations has been chose to locate in the main cities in different countries from the fast food famous restaurant's location decision. Hence, whether long or short time fast restaurant rent period to the franchisees , which can dominate the fast food restaurants' royalty and rent income. For example, if one fast food franchisee only sign one year contract to buy the fast food franchisor's loyalty to help it to sell its fast foods only one year, because it does not ensure how many fast food consumers will choose to buy these fast foods to eat, due to its price is decided by the fast food franchisor. If the cities have other fast food restaurants to let them to choose, they may find other fast food restaurants to replace it to eat fast foods very easily. If this fast good restaurant is not the most famous and it operates only short time. So, it can not earn more fast food franchisees' confidence to accept to pay long time rent to operate its fast food restaurants in cities and pay long time royalty fee to it. Otherwise, if the fast food restaurant had operated its restaurant for a long time period to raise its fast food loyalty's to let many different countries' fast food eaters to familiarize or acknowledge its fast food brand in popular. So, long fast food operation time can confirm that it has many fast food eaters, they prefer to choose to eat its fast foods. It can increase the franchisees' confidence to choose to rent its fast food restaurants and pay royalty to it in preference. Hence, the fast food franchisor's restaurant operation time whether it is long or short time, this franchisor's fast food restaurant operating time pressure factor will dominate the fast food franchisees' choices to decide to pay how long rent sand franchise royalty income to rent its restaurant to do the franchisee's fast food business in the cities locations in different countries. So, it seems that the fast food franchisor's business operation time can dominate the franchisees' choice.

In special , in fast food industry, time rich and time poor consumers behavior will dominate their fast food choices. Time rich people feel they have enough or too much time when time poor people feel time is a major constraint in their daily life. The growth of the fast food business, and the increase eating of fast food are indicators of this trend. At the same time, shorter working hours increased wealth and less pressure on domestic routine have opened up new segments of leisure consumption. But, " free time" in certain areas has not for many people, lead to an increases feeling of time richness.

So, it explains that why many fast food consumers who feel not enough time to work daily. They are time poor working people usually. So, instead of fast food taste factor influences consumer number. The people who feel time rich or poor, e.g. employment rich or poor lunch time to the employee, it will dominate the employee chooses to go to fast food restaurant in preference. So, the fast food restaurant can supply rich time to let them to eat lunch in short time, if the employee has less time to eat lunch or more tasks need him to do on that day afternoon. Hence, feeling time rich or poor to the people factor, which will dominate some consumers' choices to some kinds of businesses, such as fast food industry, or for public transportation tool choice case example, one time poor passenger feels need to go to the destination in short time. The time poor passenger will prefer to choose taxi in preference, then it is possible train or underground train, next it is tram, tain, it is bus or ferry public transportation tool choices. Otherwise, for one time rich passenger, he has more time to go to the destination. The time rich passenger will prefer to choose the cheap public transportation tool , such as bus, ferry, underground train, ferry, train. The final choice is taxi. So, passenger's time pressure will influence whose public transportation tool choice.

● Time pressure dominates consumer psychological factor

What are the factors of time pressure dominate consumer purchase psychological behaviors? How any why do this time pressure psychological factors dominate consumer behaviors? It is possible that time pressure can dominate consumer mind and behavior either choose to buy the product/ consume the service or not buy the product/consume the service. Every consumer's final purchase decision, he/she is influenced how to make by himself/herself personal psychological limited time pressure . It means that he/she will have one time maximum standard to demand himself/herself to make the final purchase decision in whose individual psychological time standard ( the consumer's individual psychological limited consumption time). So, it seems that ever consumer's final decision how he/she chooses to buy the product or consume the service, his/her consumption behavior will be dominated by whose psychological time limited consumption pressure.

So, time pressure issue seems evolutionary psychology, it looks at how consumer behavior has been affected by psychological adjustments during time pressure . It seeks to identify which consumer psychological traits are evolved through adaptations, e.g. time pressure consumption adaptations to choose the final purchase decision in the final time limited consumption pressure environment, e.g. the consumer expects this day is the final day to choose to buy what kinds of the product. If he/she can't make final purchase decision on the day, he/she will choose to buy the kind of product later, even he/she does not choose to buy the kind of product in the first or again, that is the products of natural selection, or the supermarket visitor case, he expects to choose which kind of food to eat within final 15 minutes, if he/she can't make the final decision to buy what kind of food to eat within final 15 minutes in this supermarket , or the restaurant eating consumer case, he is queueing to wait to enter the restaurant to eat. He/she expects the final queue waiting time is 15 minutes maximum. If after this 15 minutes, he/she can not be permitted to enter this restaurant, then he/she will choose to leave this restaurant and he/she will find another restaurant to replace it. So, it seems that any consumer will have himself/herself consumption limited standard time to decide whether he/she ought choose to buy any products or consume any services in any consumption environment.

Hence, the cause of consumption time pressure dominates consumer behavior, it is based on these hypothesis: Every consumer has demand characteristic and time pressure can dominate how he/she make final decision to buy or not buy any product or consume any service as well as any consumer needs have time pressure consumption demand because he/she does not expect to spend more time to choose what kinds of products to buy or what kinds of services to consume. He/she expects to make purchase or consumption final decision in short time.

IN fact, consumers will be encoded to influence how they make final purchase decision. There are three main ways in which product information can be encoded. They include: Visual ( product picture) ; for example, the consumer stores the memory by visualizing it as on product image. Aconstic ( sound); here the consumer stores the information as a sound , this explains why some consumers sometimes get the brand name( words) that sound the same mixed up when they try to remember them. Semantic ( meaning); here the object is stored in terms of what it means rather than as an image or sound, e.g. when the brand of toys can let many children feel fun to play. Then, when many parents feel familiar to the toy brand, they must remember this toy brand company is selling any kinds of toys to let children to play. So, famous brand can let consumers familiarize what products that it is selling. Such as the toy brand company can let parents feel its toys are fun to let their children to play. All these sensory information can dominate consumers make final choice purchase behavior to buy its product or consume its service in preference in any time limited pressure environment, if the brand can give positive information memory to let many customers to remember.

So, it seems that consumers are dominated to choose which kinds of products to buy or which kinds of services to consume by positive or negative emotion, time pressure in any consumption environment immediately. It is one time pressure consumption environment theory factor, it can influence consumer behavior is changed in any consumption environment time. Consequently, it explains that why time pressure can dominate consumer behaviors in possible. Also, any product seller or service provider needs to consider how to manage consumption time process to be longer to cause its consumers doe not choose to buy its product or consume its service consequently.

Methods avoid consumers
feel time pressure

In business society, it seems that any consumers will feel time pressure to cause their purchase decision making process changes in any consumption situations, when they feel time pressure either by themselves or third parties influence, e.g. not buying any thing, not consuming any service, irrational making consumption final decision etc. consumption behaviors. How to reduce their time pressure to avoid they do above consumption behaviors. I shall indicate some consumption situtations to explain how to avoid their reducing consumption , due to time pressure factor influences as below:

Firstly, I shall indicate supermarket consumption environment example. In general, supermarket visitors will expect to spend less time to visit any supermarkets to make choice to any foods. They will stay short time when they expect to buy less foods, even, they will stay more short time when they expect to buy more less foods in any supermarkets. So, any supermarkets will need to calculate their clients' limited time pressure how to influence their foods consumption number. If the supermarket visitor expects to spend maximum 20 minutes to buy any foods in the supermarket. Then, he may choose some different kinds of foods to buy, e.g. ice cream, fruit, bread, jam, fish etc. different kinds of foods, Otherwise, if the another supermarket visitor expects to spend maximum 10 minutes to buy any foods in the supermarket. Then, he may choose less different kinds of foods to compare the first one, e.g. fish, jam, ice cream only or bread, fruit , jam only. So, the second one supermarket visitor will buy less different kinds of foods, because he expects to spend 10 minutes maximum , his shopping spending time is less 10 minutes to compare the first one supermarket visitor. Because different supermarket visitor personal time pressure will limit him/her to choose more or less different kinds of foods to buy. However, time pressure will not influence every kind of foods number because every kind of food purchase number will not be influenced to buy more or less , due to the supermarket visitor personal time pressure variable factor influences his/her foods purchase number. Otherwise, the different kinds of food choice will be influenced to choose to either buy or not buy , due to every supermarket visitor personal time pressure is different.

Hence, supermarkets can focus on how to avoid any kinds of food purchase choice loses , due to supermarket consumer personal time pressure influences. In fact, in supermarket every shelf, it usually has many different brands of every kind of foods to let supermarket visitors to choose to buy. For example, the kind of jam food number has many brands are placed on shelf to let them to choose, e.g. there are more than 10 different brands of jam food are placed on one shelf. It will bring one choice problem. IF one supermarket visitor expects to choose one brand of jam within 5 minute, then he finds the shelf has more than 10 different brands of jam are placed on the shelf. Then he will feel time pressure to cause difficulty to choose the best brand of jam to buy from these 10 brands of jam. It will bring the negative emotion if he feels that all of these 10 brands of jam taste and price has no more difference. Consequently, these 10 brands of jam choice will cause he can not make the final jam purchase decision within this 5 minutes individual time limited. Anyway, if there are only 5 brands of jam are placed on this shelf, then the 5 minutes time limited consumer will has less brands of jam choices, it will influence him to do more easy choice to buy one kind of brand jam food from the shelf. It is one limited time pressure of psychological choice factor to influence any consumers feel to do any brand of food choice more easy in short time. Hence, I recommend supermarket shelf ought place every kind of food brand maximum to 5 brands , it is the best food brand number to every supermarket's shelves to let any consumers to choose different kinds of foods to make the easy food choice way in supermarket food market.

So, in super store market, it is similar to supermarket market. Super stores' main products are cloths, shoes, bags, stationaries, electronic products, e.g. fans, air conditions, televisions, radios, warmers, washing machines, dry machines, computers etc. However, super store visitors will like to spend more time to stay in any super stores, due to they feel to need more time to make purchase decision in order to make the most right choice to buy these any products. They usually expect to stay half hour , even one hour or more time in super stores. Their time pressures are depended on whether what kinds of products that they expect to buy in the super store. For example, if the super store visitor expects to buy one laptop computer. He will expect to make purchase choice decision within half hour, even more time. Otherwise, if the super store visitor expects to buy stationery, e.g. pen and rubber and pencil, he will expect to make purchase choice decision within 10 minutes. So, when the super store visitor expects to buy the product is more expensive, then his time pressure time will be longer than the super store visitor expects to buy the product is cheap, such as stationery and laptop two kinds of products.

However , due to super store 's expensive and cheap product consumers whose time pressures are different. So, brands choice number will have much different between them. For laptop example, due to superstore visitors can accept to spend longer time to make laptop purchase choice. So, one shelf can place 5 to 10 different brands of laptops , another shelf can place 5 to 10 different brands of laptops to let them to choose. Otherwise, for stationery example, due to superstore visitors can not accept to spend longer time to make stationery purchase choice. so, one shelf can place less than 5 brands of pens, the another shelf can place less than 5 brands of pencils or another shelf can place less than 5 brands of rubbers , another shelf can place less than 5 brands of rulers to let them to make purchase choice in short time. '

Secondly, for restaurant eaters example, when one restaurant has many eaters choose to enter this restaurant to eat its food, then it only chooses to let some eaters to enquire ticket number to queue to wait. Of course, some eaters will not like to wait too long time, so they will leave the queue to choose another restaurant to replace it in possible. For example, in afternoon eating time, these are two busy eaters, the student feels hurry to go to school or the working person feels hurry to go to office after lunch, although the restaurant service staff had given him one ticket to let them to queue to wait. However, their expected queue waiting time is within 15 maximum, but there are many eaters are queuing and their ticket numbers are small numbers. So, they feel that they must not enter this restaurant within 15 minutes themselves limited queue time. Consequently, their late entering this restaurant after 15 minutes issue will influence that they will choose another restaurant in possible. So, the restaurant long time queue will cause some eaters choose another restaurant in busy time. I recommend that the restaurant can limit every eater's eating time, e.g. it calculate every eater's restaurant entering time and it limits every must leave the restaurant within half hour in busy eating time. It can post notice to let them to know in the front door, e.g. Every eater needs to leave our restaurant within half hour, otherwise, you will need to bring your food to leave please. So, every eater know that they need to eat all food within half hour, otherwise, they need to bring their food to leave this restaurant. Then, this restaurant can increase more seats to let many queue waiting eaters , they do not queue to spend long time to wait to enter this restaurant. Consequently, many queue waiting eaters will choose to enter this restaurant, due to their queue waiting times are not exceed their time pressure limited time.

The final case is cinema queue . In general, any cinemas will have many audiences need to wait to buy tickets to watch movies. However, if the cinema has many audiences , they need to spend one hour, or two hours , even more than two hours to queue to wait to buy the ticket to watch any movies in the cinema. If some audiences' expected queue waiting times are within one hour. So, if these audiences' expected queue waiting time are more than one hour. Then, they will choose to leave this cinema and choose other cinemas to replace it in possible. How to avoid these time pressure audiences losing number increases in cinema busy time? I recommend that this cinema ought increase ticket purchase counter service staffs number , e.g. opening more three to five ticket purchase counters number in order to let these one hour time queue time waiting audiences can purchase ticket to watch their movies within one hour. So, opening urgent ticket purchsase service counters number issue is depended on whether there are how many audiences are waiting to buy ticket in the cinema in the time. However, it is only one best way to avoid the cinema audiences number loses in cinema busy time.

Time press how influences video playing game consumer purchase behavior

I shall explain that why it has relationship between the video game student consumer individual learning time and the working people individual working time both can influence video game playing consumer individual video game choice behavior. I shall assume that the different kinds of video game content difficult or easy win competition and entertainment spending on playing time factor will have more influence how the student or working person individual choice of what kind of video game purchase. Otherwise, every video game price and brand and video game entertainment design content will have less influence to every video game consumer individual purchase choice.

Why do the every video game's learning playing time and the playing time is spent to satisfy the feeling of winning game both factors will be the main factors to influence the feeling busy learning student or feeling rest working personal target video game playing consumer individual kind of which video game software purchase choice? Why do feeling busy learning students or feeling rest working people will be prefer to choose to buy the kinds of need spending little time to learn to play to achieve the easy winning of the video game content aim in short time?

Nowadays, the different brands of video game products have different prices, various entertainment design contents and the easy or difficult win content feeling to be promoted to sell to satisfy the students or working people video game players' entertainment needs. However, time pressure will be one important factor to influence students of working peoples' video games choices. I shall explain that the time pressure factor how will influence the feeling busy learning or feeling rest working video game players or video game content software consumers to choose to buy the kinds of video games software which can let them to feel to spend little playing and learning time and they can feel easy to win the video game competition in short time preference in this electronic entertainment video game industry.

Nowadays, video game target customers, they are young students and adult working people in common. When , the student does not need to go to school and he/she stays at home, he /she will like to play video game after he/she finishes to learn just a moment usually or the adult working person finishes jobs on the day, after he/she ate dinner, he/she will also like to play video game at home. So , video game can be one kind of entertainment product to let they feel enjoy to play when they re staying at homes.

Video game can be one kind of entertainment culture or entertainment behavior at home to them in popular. A player's ability to perform within a game entertainment is important, and players tend to knowledgeable about their achievements and failures within any game world. So, when one student hopes to get pass grade in school examination. He will choose to spend little time to attempt to win the video game content competition in short time because it can let him to feel that may increase his confidence to pass the grade in the school examination later in possible when he ensures that he had won the video game content competition. He believes that he can be trained to raise whose judgement and mind and analysis ability in his playing video game proceed. Instead of playing video game can increase student learning confidence, it can also increase the working people's confidence, when the working person hopes to be promoted or increased salary later from his supervisor's appreciation. He will attempt to spend little time to win the kind of video game content competition in short time. He will have more confident to achieve to raise his working performance to let his supervisor appreciation if he can learn how to win the kind of video game competition in short time.

It seems that whether the player needs to spend how much time to learn how to win any kind of video content game competition , this " spending learning time of winning any video content game competition in time pressure playing environment feeling factor will influence the student or working person 's video game content purchase choice. If the video game design is more complex or difficult to let the player to feel to learn to win the game competition as well as it also needs them to spend more long time to learn to play and win the kind of video content game competition. Then, it has possible to influence the hard learning students or hard working people video game consumers, they do not choose to buy any kinds of need spending long learning and playing time to win the kinds of video content game competitive software products. So, it seems that the spend how much playing and learning time to win the video game content competition factor will bring time pressure to let the hard working people or hard learning student video game consumers choose to buy the video content game software products are easy to learn to play in preference because they expect to pass grade or appreciate easy, if they feel that they can learn how to win the video game content competition in short time as well as they do not spend much playing time to win the kind of video game content competition and they will reduce their learning time at homes.

I shall explain why price won't be the main factor to influence video game players' purchase choices in preference. Some video game software sellers feel reduced sale price can attract many video game buyers' choice in preference. It is one wrong mind, due to video game software price is not too much high, it is one kind popular cheap entertainment software product. So , the kinds of similar entertainment content design video game products , their sale price difference between the kind of most expensive , the highest price video game software and the kind of the cheapest , the lowest price video game software won't be difference very much. Their price difference level may be US 410 to US\$50 or even less than US\$50 level. So,, one video fame entertainment player won't feel that the kind of similar content design of video game software's higher price which will influence he chooses to buy another cheaper similar of kind video game content design software product to replace to the prior higher price one. Because their price difference are not too much or video game software entertainment product is not on kind of expensive product to let them to feel. So, it seems what video game software price won't influence the video game players' prior one of preference choice, it is not easy to be replaced from later cheaper one, when the video game player feels like to play the kind of high price of video game content software before.

Can the video game content influence player individual purchase motivation in preference? In fact, there are many different kinds of video game contents to let players to choose. This free-to -play business model that has rapidly speed to achieve games services to general . So, some students or working people players can free download some kinds of video game software to play from online channel. It will be attractive to the no paid video game players. Hence, free download video game content will influence the paid video game players' purchase decisions for in -game content are not only affected by people's existing general attitudes, consumption values, and motivation , but also by the design decisions and the needs built into the game by the developers. Because the paid video game players won't like to buy the similar content video games, which can be free download to play from online or internet channel. They will feel unfair or not worth or loss if they choose to pay to buy the similar video game content entertainment software, after they discovered that they may be free download this kind of similar video game content to play from internet.

It will bring this question: Why will time pressure influence video game player chooses to download free video game to play in preference? When one student feels that he has no enough time to study, he won't choose to to any video game shops to do video game software comparative behavior to compare which one's price is lower, game playing content is more attractive, brand is familiar in order to make final purchase decision in preference. If he discovered that there has one kind of video game content, which can be free download to play from internet or online channel . So, when the student feels that he needs have much time to study on the day. How will choose to attempt to find some kind of video game contents from computer tool which has the attractive entertainment content , it can let he to feel enjoy to play and it is free download from mobile or computer. Then, he won't choose to spend non predictive time to visit any video game shops to make purchase decision on that day. So, time pressure will be one factor to influence some video game software consumers to feel whether they ought either visit any video game shops to make purchase choice or download some free video game contents at homes for the feeling no enough learning time student players. Even time pressure will also influence adult working people video game players, when the working person feels tries after his full day busy working on that day. Then, he will want to stay at home to rest . Although, he expects to visit any video game shops to choose which video game software product(s) to buy on that day, but when he discovered that there are some video game contents which are attractive to influence him to do free download behavior from internet at home. Also, he feels very tried and he will choose to stay at home on that day. If he can find some free video game contents are attractive to influence he chooses to do free download video game contents behavior and replace visiting video game stores behavior on that day. So, free download video game content entertainment activity will be one attractive promotion video game software method to assist the video game sellers' new video game products to let many feeling time pressure learning or working video game players to know from internet channel.

Consequently, online free entertainment video game content download playing choice will influence many video game shops will lose many feeling time pressure video game players number every day in possible. Also, it means that the lazy students or disliking learning students or no job people or ( less working hours) part time working people, they will be the main target video game customers, due to they accept to spend much time to visit their video game shops to choose any kinds of video game software to buy in preference.

● How can video game advertisement method influence feeling time pressure and feeling without time pressure video game software consumer purchase ?

In fact, video game sellers can choose new media channel to advertise their new video game software products, e.g. computer online advertisement channel, instead of video game pictures in shops, magazine, newspapers, television, radio ,cinema, public transportation tools poster traditional advertisement channels. However, computer online advertisement channel can attract many feeling learning time pressure of students consumers and feeling lack of enough rest time working people consumers to let them to choose to view their video game software advertisements from online websites at homes conveniently.

It is easy to understand , due to these feeling lack of enough learning time student video game players and feeling lack enough rest time working people video game players, they go back home after they finished learning in schools or they finished jobs in workplaces on that video game purchase planning day. After they eat their dinners, they may turn on computers to search information from internet. Suddenly, they discover some attractive video game contents photos or images are advertised from the video game seller's website or public yahoo website , even they can choose to buy any one of these video game software from online shopping channel. Then, they will feel convenient to buy any one of these video game software from internet channel. SO, online video game advertisement will be the feeling time pressure video game players' first time contact channel at homes or the fastest advertisement contact channel to compare visiting video game store post advertisement, television , radio , magazine contact advertisement channels, when they are staying at homes.

Due to internet is popular to be used to search any information for consumers. So, the traditional magazine, newspapers, television, radio and visiting video game stores advertisement channels won't be more attractive to the feeling time pressure video game consumers . They will choose to find any information from internet at homes in preference , when they have at least one computer to use at home, they can click website to search any information from internet easily.

The most important factor is that they can feel to spend little time to search information from internet to compare spending more time to find anywhere places whether they has magazines or book stores to sell video game magazine and newspapers publishers, radios and television won't inform them when they have video game advertisements to let they know whether what new video game software will promote to sell as soon as possible when they buy newspapers or turn on radios or televisions at home.

Otherwise, internet will be easy to let the feeling pressure video game software consumers to know when whose liking new video content game software(s) will be promoted to sell from internet advertisement easily. Also, the feeling time pressure video software consumers can choose to buy their liking video game software (s) from online shopping channel in possible if the video game seller can provide one website to let him/her to pay visa to buy and then it can deliver the video game software(s) to his/ her home immediately or tomorrow or later time when the buyer's home located in overseas or far away from the video game seller's warehouse and their software are needed to be delivered by air plane transportation.

So, the feeling time pressure video game players won't need to leave their homes to spend more time to visit any video game stores to make final video game purchase decision any time. Hence, online advertisement and shopping channel will be one good sale promotion method to any feeling time pressure video game players nowadays. It will influence the traditional visiting video game stores' video game consumers' purchase behaviors to change to online purchase behaviors at homes conveniently, because they avoid to waste much time to visit video game stores as well as avoid to waste much time to choose any video game products in different video game stores, when they are staying in different video game stores. Visiting video game purchase behavior will need they spend whole day time to make final purchase choice, even it is possible that they can not make any video game software purchase decision after they visit many video game stores on that day.

Otherwise , online game advertisement channel can let them to feel to spend little time to search any new video game contents from every web page as well as every web page can show the new video game content images or photos or pictures to let every online users to see clearly when he/she sits down to turn on computer to search any kinds of video game content information to view at home in short time.

In conclusion, online video game advertisement and online shopping channel can attract many feeling time pressure video game players' consideration when they need to search any kinds of new or old video game contents information and it also changes their purchase decision to online shopping from traditional visiting video game store shopping behavior. Video game industry's advertisement method , sale method is the kind of video game playing content's easy or difficult feeling degree , spending how much playing time to win the competition in the game entertainment environment factors will influence the feeling time pressure video game players' final purchase decision making choice behavior to any video game software publishers nowadays.

Time pressure consumption or production situation explanation

Will one consumer feel difficult to make consumption choice or one employee feel pressure to work when the worker works in the company's high pressure productive environment or the consumer makes difficult purchase choice in high pressure consumption environment? Will time pressure bring motivation to the consumer purchase decision or the employee working efficiency? It depends on some factors to either cause time pressure working environment or raise the employee individual efficiency , or time pressure consumption environment can either encourage the consumer purchase decision or discourage the consumer purchase decision . I shall explain as below:

What does efficiency mean? Due to economic problem is a scarcity of resource, efficiency is concerns with the optimal production, consumption environment. For time pressure consumption situation example, e.g. supermarket shopping counter check out purchase queue waiting time pressure, cinema purchase ticket queue waiting time pressure, restaurant queue waiting booking table time pressure etc. different consumption pressure time waiting situation. For time pressure working situation example, e.g. supervisor's demand tasks finishing on time before the employee leaves the office on the day, then the supervisor's demand will cause the employee feels time pressure to do all tasks on time, otherwise, he needs to work overtime, even no extra allowance compensation to his extra time loss, or the employee needs to do another employee's tasks , due to he is absent on the day. However, this situation can be called economically efficient production or consumption if: no one can be worse off, no additional output can be obtained, without increasing the amount of inputs, production proceeds at the lowest possible per unit cost. For these economic efficient consumption situation example, the consumer has much time to wait, the shop has less different styles of products to let them to spend time to choose in the shop's shelf.

However, these definitions of efficiency are not exactly equivalent, but all they are caused by the idea that a system is efficient if nothing more than be achieved given the resources available. On time pressure working environment influence aspect, Time pressure working environment may bring efficiency, but time pressure working environment may also bring inefficiency, e.g. employing workers who are not necessary for the productive process. For example, a firm may be more concerned about the political implications of making people redundant than getting rid of surplus workers, or lack of management control, if a firm does not have supervision of workers, then productivity may tall as workers talk it easy, not finding cheapest suppliers, a firm may continue to source raw materials from a high cost supplier rather than look for cheaper raw materials to be supplied to let workers to work in one short time task finishing environment. Then, they may feel short time task finishing pressure to bring inefficiency production result.

I shall indicate efficient production and efficient consumption situations as below:

For building a new airport working time pressure situation example, how to evaluate that it is one efficient productive situation. When a new airport may lead a greater increase in social benefit than social cost. It seems that an efficient productive situation in time pressure working environment. The time pressure can excite or encourage workers hard to work and the won't feel pressure to work to cause inefficient performance. Therefore, these is a net gain to society. However, those people living near the new building airport will lost out. Therefore, this is not an improvement. However , if the people living nearby were compensated for extra noise, when the workers need to use equipment build the new airport in the pressure building time when they feel lack of enough equipment supplies or lack of enough workers to cooperate to work. Then, it is possible to have a negative improvement inefficient production. So, how to evaluate whether the new airport builders feel time pressure to finish this new airport building project before the due date or not. It can depend on whether the people living near the new airport often listen noise or not. In a without time pressure working situation, the workers do not need often to cause noise in their airport production process. If they feel no time pressure to finish this new airport building project before the finishing due date. Their working behaviors ought not often cause noise to influence themselves nervous or emotion to be poor to work, or feeling workload to bring the inefficient performance consequence to finish this new airport after the due date in possible. It ought seem that they won't feel time pressure and they have confidence to finish to build this new airport before the due date. If the employer has enough workers number and equipment supplies number to let them to do this new airport building task. Otherwise, if they need to often cause noise. It implies that it has no enough workers number and equipment number to let them to build this new airport before the due date. They feel time pressure to finish this new airport building project. So , the employer ought increase workers and equipment to reduce their worry about on building this new airport project before or one due date finishing, if the employer hoped that they can perform efficiently.

For avoiding feeling time pressure on consumption situation example, when the product can be allocated efficiency, then consumers will feel less time pressure consumption psychological influence. This occurs when products and services are distributed according to consumer choice preferences. It means that the seller can make more accurate preferable choice prediction whether consumers will choose to buy what kinds of styles of products or characteristics of services provision in preference. So, they won't need to spend more time to do choices to decide whether which styles of products or characteristics of service provisions whom hope to buy or consume in preference.

In one allocative efficient occurs when the price of the product or service is same to the marginal cost. A more precise definition of allocation efficiency is at an output level where the price equals the marginal cost of production . This is because the price that consumers are willing to pay is equal to the marginal utility that they get. Therefore, the optimal distribution is achieved when the marginal utility of products equals the marginal cost. For example , when firms in perfect competition are said to product at an allocative efficient level, monopolies can increase price above the marginal cost of production and are allocative inefficient. So, if the product is sold in the monopolies market environment. Many the similar product sellers raise sale price to sell similar styles of products to let consumers to choose to make purchase decision. Then, will influence them to feel their choices to the kinds of similar styles of products in the time pressure product choice consumption situation. Otherwise, firms are in the perfect competitive consumption environment. Consumers can feel their similar product prices are not difference too much. Then, they will feel less time pressure to make which kinds of product choice of purchase decision in preference. They will spend less time to make final purchase decision. So, whether the kind of product market is monopolies or perfect competition which will influence consumers feel more or less time pressure consumption generally. Consequently, consumer time pressure feeling and the kind of product 's market environment, they have close relationship to influence consumer purchase decision making behavior.

What is dynamic efficient production environment? This refers to efficient over time. Dynamic efficiency involves the introduction of new technology and working methods to reduce costs over time, e.g. letting workers feel that productive time can be reduce to produce the same level of tasks. Then, they can avoid long time pressure to influence their working performance. With this mind, we can define dynamic efficiency as an aspect of economic efficiency that measures the speed or the rate at which the production possibility curve moves from one static equilibrium point to another within a given period. For Ford Motor company efficient production predictive method case example, in the 1920 year, the Ford Motor factor were very efficient for that particular year. However, compared to later decades, we can not say that the production methods of the 1920 year were efficient. On other words, it is important for firms to make best use of given resources. But, they also need to develop greater use of resources over time. Hence, Ford Motor can let workers to avoid time pressure feeling to produce its any motor vehicles i their productive process in 1920 year. When its new productive technology is adopted to be used to manufacture any kinds of its more vehicles in factory. Also, it can raise their productive efficiency to manufacture any motor vehicles in 1920 year. However, although Ford Motor can make best use of given resources to assist workers to produce any kinds of motor vehicles efficiently. The vehicle buyers' driving needs or new design motor demands are increasing. They need new different kinds of Ford Motor design to be provided to let them to choose. So, Ford Motor also needs to develop greater use of more resources over time, due to the more different styles of new design motor vehicles are needed. So, the new kinds of productive resources are needed to be develop in order to adopt to vehicle buyers' needs. If Ford Motor can not find or discover any new productive material and it can not innovate any new kinds of productive methods to be taught to let workers to learn how to manufacture the future new designs of Ford Motor vehicles efficiently. Then, they wil be possible to feel time pressure to work, due to they can not adopt how to manufacture the future new design motor vehicles, when they are not proficient to apply the future new productive technology to manufacture any new design of motor vehicles.

This is one good example to explain high technological manufacturing resources and techniques and method can let workers to reduce time pressure to manufacture in their manufacturing process, but if the manufacturer can not improve its manufacturing technology to let its workers can continue adapt how to apply the new different manufacturing method to manufacture the future new design or innovative products. Then, they will be possible that they feel time manufacturing pressure and raising inefficient manufacturing performance, due to the manufacturing technology or productive technique can not be improved and training to them to raise skillful proficiency. So, these productive workers will onle reduce time pressure to manufacture in short time, if the manufacturer can not improve any new kinds of manufacturing techniques and teach them how to apply the future new manufacturing techniques to work efficiently. .Then, their performance will be ppor in possible when they feel long time pressure o work in the long time pressure working environment. Hence, it has relationship between new technique improvement and long or short time working pressure and performance.

Distributive efficiency can raise consumption desire and it can reduce consumer individual choice time to make purchase decision in short time.

Concerned with allocating products and services provision according to who needs them most . Therefore, requires an equitable distribution . Distributive efficiency occurs when products sale and service provision are consumed by those who need them most. Distributive efficiency is concerned with an equitable distribution of resources because of the law of diminishing marginal returns .

The law of diminishing marginal returns states that as consumption of product increase the product users tend to get diminishing marginal utility. For example, if a family already has three cars, but gets a fourth car, this fourth car will only increase this family net utility by a small amount. If by constrast someone on a low income is able to get their first car, the marginal utility will be much higher. Therefore, to be distributive efficient, society will need to ensure an equitable distribution of resources. For car sale case example, if the car seller has distribution of resource, such as different styles of car kinds sale number efficiently, e.g. the high quality expensive car number manufacturing number is less than the low quality cheap car number. Then, there are many low income people may have enough time too pay to buy the cheap car in the car sale market. Then, it is possible that the car company can sell more cheap cars in short time, due to many low income people do not need to spend long time to consider whether they ought buy or not buy any first car, even another car or other cars for their family to drive. They will not feel purchase time pressure to make final car purchase choice, due to there are many common low quality cheap cars number are supplied to be sold in the country's car market immediately. So, when the car company can concentrate on manufacturing many low quality cheap cars to prepare to sell. Although, its high quality expensive car number reduces, and it will increase its high profit earn in possible in short time only. Otherwise, in long time benefit aspect, many low quality cheap cars sale number will increase many low income car buyers nu,bers when they find the car manufacturer can have many different style design of low quality cheap cars to let them to choose more than other car competitors in the country's car sale market.

In long time, it will reduce time purchase choice pressure to its car consumers, when many car buyers believe this car company only it has many different styles of design low quality and cheap price cars to let them to choose to buy to compare other brands of car companies in whose country. Then, they won't feel need to spend extra much time to choose other brands of cars to compare this car company's cars. It implies that the country car buyers only consider to spend less time to choose this brand of any cars to make car purchase decision in preference. They won't feel time pressure to consider other brands of any kinds of style cars purchase choices often habitually.

So, this brand cars have built choice habit to many low quality and cheap car buyers in this country. So, when the seller can build long time brand of any this car company's any car products choice habit to let many buyers this brand cars are preferable choice, then they will prefer to spend short time to make purchase decision for this company's any cars . Then it can sell any low quality and cheap cars to compare other brands of car companies more easily.